TRIANGLE TRICKS

ONE EASY UNIT, DOZENS OF GORGEOUS QUILTS

INTRODUCTION BY SALLY SCHNEIDER

Martingale™
& COMPANY

Triangle Tricks: One Easy Unit, Dozens of
    Gorgeous Quilts
© 2003 Martingale & Company

& C O M P A N Y

That
Patchwork
Place®

20205 144th Avenue NE
Woodinville, WA 98072-8478
www.martingale-pub.com

Printed in China
08 07 06 05 04 03   8 7 6 5 4 3 2 1

▲ ▲ ▲ ▲ ▲ ▲ ▲ ▲ ▲ ▲ ▲ ▲ ▲ ▲ ▲ ▲ ▲

MISSION STATEMENT
We are dedicated to providing quality products and
service by working together to inspire creativity
and to enrich the lives we touch.

▼ ▼ ▼ ▼ ▼ ▼ ▼ ▼ ▼ ▼ ▼ ▼ ▼ ▼ ▼ ▼ ▼

CREDITS
President . . . . Nancy J. Martin
CEO. . . . . Daniel J. Martin
Publisher . . . . Jane Hamada
Editorial Director. . . . . Mary V. Green
Managing Editor . . . . Tina Cook
Technical Editor . . . . Karen Costello Soltys
Editorial Assistant . . . . Laurie Bevan
Copy Editor . . . . Liz McGehee
Design Director . . . . Stan Green
Cover Designer . . . . Regina Girard
Text Designer . . . . Jennifer LaRock Shontz
Photographer. . . . . Brent Kane
Illustrator . . . . Robin Strobel

Library of Congress Cataloging-in-Publication Data

Triangle tricks.
        p. cm.
    ISBN 1-56477-467-8
    1. Patchwork—Patterns. 2. Patchwork quilts.
    TT835 .T764 2003
    746.46'041—dc21
                                2002152794

CONTENTS

▼▼▼▼▼▼▼▼▼▼▼▼

INTRODUCTION

▼▼▼▼▼▼▼▼▼▼▼▼▼▼▼▼▼

Ideas come to different people in different ways—and sometimes at strange times. I think there are lots of good ideas floating out there somewhere; sometimes when they land, they get ignored, but sometimes they hit pay dirt. That's the way the technique I call "Mary's Triangles" came to me almost twenty years ago.

I was skiing with my friend Mary Kelleher, and from out of the blue, I got the idea for a shortcut technique to make Shaded Four Patch blocks. I was so excited that I just couldn't stop talking about it to Mary as we rode up the ski lift. I even asked her for a pencil and paper so that I could draw it, but, of course, she didn't have any. She suggested that I draw it in the snow, and that's where I drafted my first Mary's Triangles block! I named my technique after Mary because, even though she doesn't quilt, she is a most encouraging friend.

Back then, I called the technique Mary's Baskets, because all I could think to make from the Shaded Four Patch blocks were Basket blocks. But after playing with blocks for a while, I came up with so many different ways to put the blocks together that I realized baskets were much too limited an application. From then on, I've called my concept "Mary's Triangles."

Today, Mary's Triangles is the featured technique in *Triangle Tricks*. Laurie Bevan of Martingale & Company fell in love with my original technique and quickly saw that it held many possibilities. But she was unsatisfied that the previously published directions were for making the blocks in only two sizes: 4" x 4" and 5" x 5". With so many uses for this block, Laurie didn't want to be limited to using the technique to make just these block sizes. So, she calculated the sizes you need to cut to make Mary's Triangles blocks in sizes ranging from 2" to 12"—and half sizes, too!

Laurie's enthusiasm over this fun technique quickly spread around the Martingale & Company offices, and soon, everyone was making quilts using the method, which led to the idea for this book. In it, you'll find Laurie's handy cutting charts, so at a glance, you can make any size block you want. You can even mix and match different sizes or use smaller-size triangle units inside of larger ones. You'll find ten quilt projects, some made by Martingale folk, some made by my friends and fellow quilting teachers, and even two by me. There's also a wonderful gallery of quilt photos to spark your creativity even more.

The possibilities for using Mary's Triangles seem just about limitless! With so many terrific quilts you can make using my simple shortcut technique, I know that once you've tried it, you won't be able to stop at just one.

Sally Schneider

THE BASIC BLOCK

▼ ▼ ▼ ▼ ▼ ▼ ▼ ▼ ▼ ▼ ▼ ▼ ▼ ▼ ▼ ▼ ▼ ▼ ▼

Just what is a Mary's Triangles block? It's a familiar quilt block, which is also called Flying Goose and Shaded Four Patch, that's made using a shortcut technique. The technique is a simple one, and you can complete dozens of blocks in just a few hours. In this book, you'll find projects made with two different variations of the block. Block A features a large triangle on one side and a square surrounded by small triangles on the other side. Block B contains only triangles.

Block A   Block B

The beauty of the Mary's Triangles technique is that you don't actually cut and sew triangles! There's no fussing with matching points, sewing on cut bias edges that can stretch, or keeping your fingers crossed that all your blocks will turn out the same size. By starting with easy-to-cut squares and rectangles, you can quickly sew units that turn into two blocks for the work of one.

MAKING BLOCK A

Let's start with Block A. The sewing steps are easy, and you can make your finished blocks in any size you like. (The cutting chart gives 21 different block sizes!) For each pair of finished blocks, you need to start with two squares, two small rectangles, and one large rectangle. Refer to the "Cutting Sizes for Block A" chart on page 10 to locate the sizes you need to cut for your desired finished-size blocks. Cut the shapes, and you're ready to make your blocks.

1. Sew the squares to the small rectangles.

    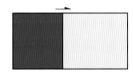

   Make 2.
   Press toward rectangle.

2. Sew the pair of square/rectangle units together as shown. Be sure to match the outside edges.

   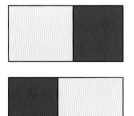 

3. Clip the seam allowance just through the seam line in the space between the two squares. From the wrong side, press the seams away from the squares, changing the direction of the seam at the center cut. There will be a small hole in the unit where you clipped, but you will eventually be cutting through this hole and it will not appear in your finished blocks.

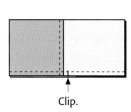

Clip.

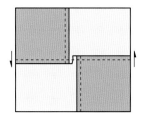

Press seams away from squares.

4. You can use either a ruler or a template for marking the sewing line on the pieced unit. If you prefer to use a template, make one by cutting a square of template plastic in the required size (see the chart on page 10). Cut the template in half diagonally.

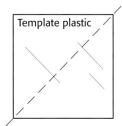

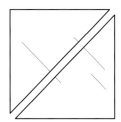

5. To mark the sewing line, place the template on the wrong side of your pieced rectangle, with the corner of the template on the square. Draw the diagonal line as shown below. Place the template on the opposite corner, again with the corner of the template on the square. Mark a second sewing line.

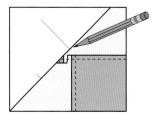
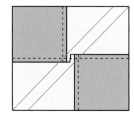

Mark stitching lines.

▷ Note: If you prefer, you can mark the sewing lines quickly and easily with a ruler. See the "Alternate Marking Method" sidebar on the opposite page.

6. Place the large rectangle, right sides together, with the pieced rectangle. Pin them together in the corners opposite the marked lines to secure their position. Sew on each of the lines you drew, and then cut between the lines with a rotary cutter or scissors to make two blocks as shown. Press the seam allowances toward the large triangles.

▷ Note: The seam allowance will be greater than ¼" wide. If you prefer to have exact ¼" seams, you can trim them to the correct size using your rotary cutter and ruler.

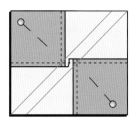
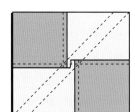

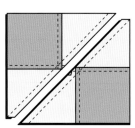

Makes 2.

ALTERNATE MARKING METHOD

To mark sewing lines, you can bypass the template and simply use your rotary-cutting ruler for this task.

You'll need a ruler that has a 45° line on it. You can use a square ruler if its side is longer than the diagonal measurement of the block, or you can use a long rectangular ruler.

1. Place the pieced unit on your table with the wrong side up and the small square or triangle square in the upper left corner. Place the ruler on the block so the 45° line is aligned with the edge of the block. Align the ruler so that its edge intersects the top corner of the block and the intersection of the small square's seams. Mark the stitching line.

45° line

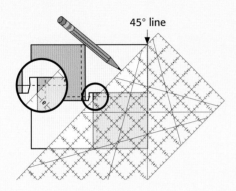

2. To draw the second stitching line, scoot the ruler up so that it aligns with the other small square or triangle square and the bottom left corner. Then mark the stitching line as described above.

To complete the blocks, stitch on the lines and cut between them as described in step 6 for Block A and step 8 for Block B.

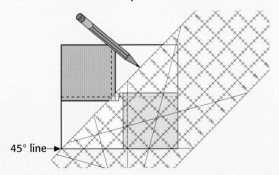

45° line→

MAKING BLOCK B

Block B is made much like Block A, except that you need to make triangle squares first. These take the place of the plain squares used in Block A. Although these blocks will take a little longer to complete because of the time needed to make the triangle squares, they give you new design options for your quilt.

1. Place the two squares (one background and one contrast print) right sides together. On the back of the lighter square, draw a diagonal line from one corner to the opposite corner.

2. Stitch ¼" from each side of the line. Cut the squares on the drawn line, and then press the seams of the resulting triangle squares toward the darker fabric. Trim the dog ears from the corners. Repeat to make one triangle square for each block in your quilt.

Stitch.   Cut.   Press.
                              Trim corners.

3. Using an accurate ¼"-wide seam allowance, sew the triangle squares to the small rectangles. Make sure the darker triangle is facing in the direction shown.

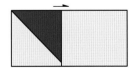

▷ **Note:** In some of the projects, the color placement is changed from this traditional arrangement, but instructions are given to make the changes necessary to create the quilt shown.

4. Sew the pair of triangle-square/rectangle units together as shown. Be sure to match the outside edges.

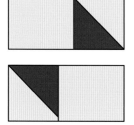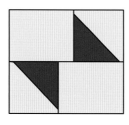

5. Clip the seam allowance just through the seam line in the space between the two triangle squares. Pressing from the wrong side, press the seams away from the triangle squares. There will be a small hole in the unit where you clipped, but you will eventually be cutting through this hole and it will not appear in your finished block.

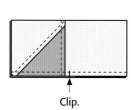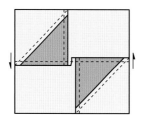

Clip.

Press seams away
from triangles.

6. You can use either a ruler or a template for marking the sewing line on the pieced unit. If you prefer to use a template, make one by cutting a square of template plastic in the required size (see the "Cutting Sizes for Block B" chart on page 11). Cut the template in half diagonally.

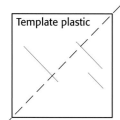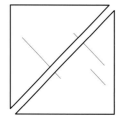

7. To mark the sewing line, place the template on the wrong side of your pieced rectangle, with the corner of the template on the triangle square. Draw the diagonal line as shown below. Place the template on the opposite corner, again with the corner of the template on the triangle square. Mark a second sewing line.

If you prefer, you can mark the sewing lines with a ruler, referring to the directions in "Alternate Marking Method" on page 7.

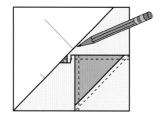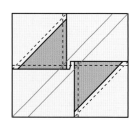

Mark stitching lines.

8. Place a large rectangle of dark fabric, right sides together, with each pieced rectangle. Sew on each of the lines you drew, and then cut between them. Press the seam allowances toward the large triangles. You will have two blocks as shown.

Note: The seam allowance will be greater than ¼". If you prefer to have exact ¼" seams, you can trim them to the correct size.

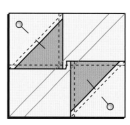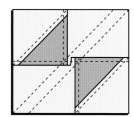

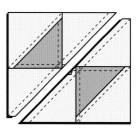

Makes 2.

PINWHEEL OPTION

By rotating the triangle-square position in Block B, you can make triangle units that form pinwheels when four are arranged together. Simply follow the illustrations below for the correct placement and voilà—you'll have pinwheel blocks!

  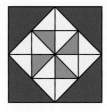

Detail of pinwheel option from
"Starring Mary's Triangles"

CUTTING SIZES FOR BLOCK A

Determine the finished size of block you want to make for your project, and then read across to see what size to cut the pieces. Divide the number of blocks you need by two to determine how many sets of squares and rectangles you'll need to cut. One set of two squares, two small rectangles, and one large rectangle make two blocks.

FINISHED BLOCK SIZE	SQUARE (Cut 2)	SMALL RECTANGLE (Cut 2)	LARGE RECTANGLE (Cut 1)	MARKING TEMPLATE (Template is optional)
2"	1½"	1½" x 2½"	2½" x 3½"	2½" ◿
2½"	1¾"	1¾" x 2¾"	3" x 4"	3" ◿
3"	2"	2" x 3"	3½" x 4½"	3½" ◿
3½"	2¼"	2¼" x 3¼"	4" x 5"	4" ◿
4"	2½"	2½" x 3½"	4½" x 5½"	4½" ◿
4½"	2¾"	2¾" x 3¾"	5" x 6"	5" ◿
5"	3"	3" x 4"	5½" x 6½"	5½" ◿
5½"	3¼"	3¼" x 4¼"	6" x 7"	6" ◿
6"	3½"	3½" x 4½"	6½" x 7½"	6½" ◿
6½"	3¾"	3¾" x 4¾"	7" x 8"	7" ◿
7"	4"	4" x 5"	7½" x 8½"	7½" ◿
7½"	4¼"	4¼" x 5¼"	8" x 9"	8" ◿
8"	4½"	4½" x 5½"	8½" x 9½"	8½" ◿
8½"	4¾"	4¾" x 5¾"	9" x 10"	9" ◿
9"	5"	5" x 6"	9½" x 10½"	9½" ◿
9½"	5¼"	5¼" x 6¼"	10" x 11"	10" ◿
10"	5½"	5½" x 6½"	10½" x 11½"	10½" ◿
10½"	5¾"	5¾" x 6¾"	11" x 12"	11" ◿
11"	6"	6" x 7"	11½" x 12½"	11½" ◿
11½"	6¼"	6¼" x 7¼"	12" x 13"	12" ◿
12"	6½"	6½" x 7½"	12½" x 13½"	12½" ◿

Determine the finished size of block you want to make for your project, and then read across to see what size to cut the pieces. Divide the number of blocks you need by two to determine how many sets of squares and rectangles you'll need to cut. One set of two squares, two small rectangles, and one large rectangle make two blocks.

FINISHED BLOCK SIZE	SQUARE (Cut 2)*	SMALL RECTANGLE (Cut 2)	LARGE RECTANGLE (Cut 1)	MARKING TEMPLATE (Template is optional)
2"	1⅞"	1½" x 2½"	2½" x 3½"	2½"
2½"	2⅛"	1¾" x 2¾"	3" x 4"	3"
3"	2⅜"	2" x 3"	3½" x 4½"	3½"
3½"	2⅝"	2¼" x 3¼"	4" x 5"	4"
4"	2⅞"	2½" x 3½"	4½" x 5½"	4½"
4½"	3⅛"	2¾" x 3¾"	5" x 6"	5"
5"	3⅜"	3" x 4"	5½" x 6½"	5½"
5½"	3⅝"	3¼" x 4¼"	6" x 7"	6"
6"	3⅞"	3½" x 4½"	6½" x 7½"	6½"
6½"	4⅛"	3¾" x 4¾"	7" x 8"	7"
7"	4⅜"	4" x 5"	7½" x 8½"	7½"
7½"	4⅝"	4¼" x 5¼"	8" x 9"	8"
8"	4⅞"	4½" x 5½"	8½" x 9½"	8½"
8½"	5⅛"	4¾" x 5¾"	9" x 10"	9"
9"	5⅜"	5" x 6"	9½" x 10½"	9½"
9½"	5⅝"	5¼" x 6¼"	10" x 11"	10"
10"	5⅞"	5½" x 6½"	10½" x 11½"	10½"
10½"	6⅛"	5¾" x 6¾"	11" x 12"	11"
11"	6⅜"	6" x 7"	11½" x 12½"	11½"
11½"	6⅝"	6¼" x 7¼"	12" x 13"	12"
12"	6⅞"	6½" x 7½"	12½" x 13½"	12½"

* Cut one square of background fabric and one of a contrasting fabric.

CLEVER DESIGN OPTIONS

As exciting as the simple block construction is, the real fun starts when you begin arranging the triangle blocks. You can probably put your blocks together in hundreds of ways, so when you complete yours, spend some time at the design wall trying several different arrangements. Even if you've started out with a particular plan in mind, you may be surprised at the effects you can create by turning your blocks in new arrangements.

SETTING IDEAS

You can make up your own setting, but if you need a place to start or some inspiration, begin with traditional Log Cabin settings. Any design customarily used to set Log Cabin blocks, which are typically half dark/half light split along the diagonal, will work for your Mary's Triangles blocks.

Some common settings are shown below. Straight Furrows emphasizes diagonal lines. Sunshine and Shadow (or Barn Raising) settings create a large diamond pattern in the center. Streak of Lightning and its many variations create zigzag patterns across the quilt top, while rotating the blocks will make pinwheels appear.

Straight Furrows

Pinwheels

Sunshine and Shadow Variations

Streak of
Lightning

Streak of Lightning Variations

BLOCK IDEAS

While the Mary's Triangles block is great on its own, it has many other applications, too. First of all, take a look through a book of quilt blocks. You'll find that the basic Mary's Triangles block is often a component of traditional pieced blocks. Instead of cutting lots of triangles for these blocks, simply piece the units as described in "The Basic Block" on page 5 for an easy way to whip up a batch of blocks in a hurry. Below are some traditional quilt blocks with the Mary's Triangles units highlighted.

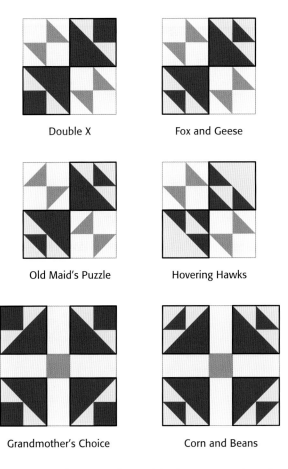

Double X

Fox and Geese

Old Maid's Puzzle

Hovering Hawks

Grandmother's Choice

Corn and Beans

You can also expand your block repertoire by adapting a traditional block that is made of triangle squares. Simply replace the triangle squares with Mary's Triangles units. Some favorite choices for makeovers are simple blocks that are arranged four squares across by four squares down. See how the triangle units add sparkle? And while the blocks look complex, you now know just how easy it is to make them!

Here are just three possibilities of traditional blocks you can take from plain to pizzazz with the help of Mary's Triangles. Rather than cutting individual pieces, refer to the charts on pages 10 and 11 to find the sizes you need to cut. Then use the Mary's Triangles technique to make those parts of the block.

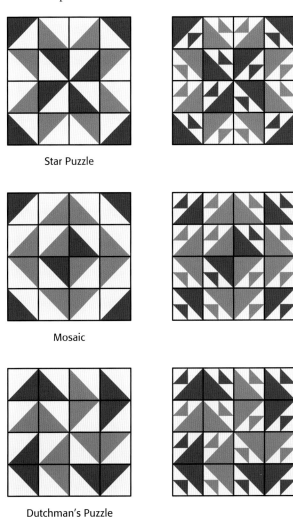

Star Puzzle

Mosaic

Dutchman's Puzzle

Even the Mary's Triangles block can be spiced up by using a small Mary's Triangles block in place of the small square. Simply make one small Mary's Triangles block for each full-size block you need. Use a 3" finished block to substitute for the plain square in a 6" finished block, a 4½" block for the square in a 9" finished block, and so on.

THE PROJECTS

By Margaret E. J. LaBenne, Hendersonville, North Carolina, 2002.
Finished Quilt Size: 73½" x 89½". Block used: 4" Block A.

If the homespun corner is your favorite part of the quilt shop, this is the perfect project for you. Of course, you could substitute any favorite fabric collection for the plaids. Whatever your fancy, using fat quarters will give you a good variety to make a scrappy mix of Mary's Triangles blocks. If you pay careful attention to your block layout, the hearts will appear around the edges of the quilt setting. And by adding a few blocks in the pieced border, you'll complete the Barn Raising pattern.

~ Marge LaBenne

MATERIALS

Yardage is based on 42"-wide fabric unless otherwise noted.

14 or more fat quarters (18" x 20") assorted dark homespun plaids for blocks

8 or more fat quarters assorted light homespun plaids for blocks

2¼ yds. red homespun plaid for outer border

⅝ yd. light homespun plaid for middle border

⅝ yd. navy homespun plaid for inner border

5¾ yds. backing fabric

¾ yd. binding fabric

78" x 94" piece of batting

CUTTING

All measurements include ¼"-wide seam allowances.

From *each* of the 14 dark fat quarters, cut:

    2 strips, 5½" x 20"; crosscut each strip into 4 rectangles, 4½" x 5½"

    2 strips, 2½" x 20"; crosscut each strip into 8 squares, 2½" x 2½"

From *each* of the 8 light fat quarters, cut:

    6 strips, 2½" x 20"; crosscut each strip into 5 rectangles, 2½" x 3½"

From *each* of the light and navy homespun border fabrics, cut:

    4 inner border strips, 2½" x 24½"

    4 inner border strips, 2½" x 16½"

From the red homespun border fabric, cut on the lengthwise grain:

    2 outer border strips, 9" x 73½"

    2 outer border strips, 9" x 72½"

From the binding fabric, cut:

    9 strips, 2½" x 42"

BLOCK ASSEMBLY

You need 212 of Block A (see page 5) for this quilt. Mix the dark and light fabrics for a scrappy look.

1. Sew a dark 2½" square to each light 2½" x 3½" rectangle. Press the seams toward the dark squares.

 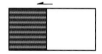

Make 212.

2. Sew the pieced strips into pairs as shown, with the dark squares on opposite ends.

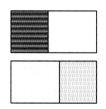 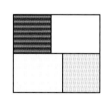

Mix lights and darks for a scrappy look.

3. Clip the seam allowances to the seam line between the dark squares. Press the seam away from the dark squares, changing the direction of the seam at the center cut.

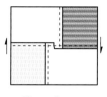

Clip and press.

4. Pair the units from step 3 with the 4½" x 5½" dark rectangles, and refer to "The Basic Block" on page 5 to mark, sew, and cut the units. Open the blocks and press the seams toward the dark triangle.

5. Repeat steps 1–4 to make 212 blocks.

QUILT TOP ASSEMBLY

1. Lay out the blocks as shown in 8 rows of 6 blocks each. Follow the diagram carefully to get the direction of the large triangles in the correct positions.

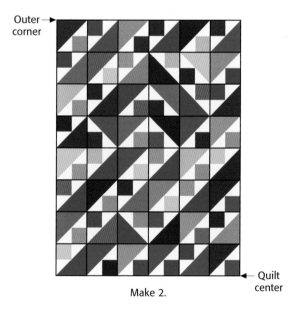

Make 2.

2. Sew the blocks together in rows, and then sew the rows together to complete one quadrant of the quilt. Repeat to make a second identical panel.

▷ **Note:** The block placement needs to be identical, but the color combinations may vary.

3. For the other two quadrants of the quilt, you need to make mirror-image panels of the ones you've just pieced. Lay out the blocks as shown in 8 rows of 6 blocks each. Sew the blocks together in rows, and then sew the rows together. Repeat to make a second panel in the same manner. Note that you will have 20 blocks left over to use for the borders.

Make 2.

4. Sew the light (middle) and navy (inner) border strips together in pairs, one light strip to one navy strip of the same length. Press the seams toward the navy fabric.

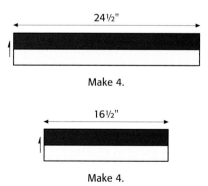

24½"

Make 4.

16½"

Make 4.

5. Sew 2 blocks to one end of each of the longer strip sets. Carefully check the position of the large triangles to be sure they are placed as shown. Make a total of 4 long border strips, 2 of each as shown.

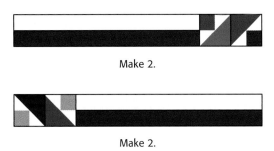

Make 2.

Make 2.

6. Sew the long strip sets to the long outer side of the panels, so the navy fabric is joined to the patchwork, and the pieced blocks are at the center edge of the quilt as shown, not at the top or bottom.

← Quilt center

7. Sew 2 blocks to one end of each of the shorter strip sets. Add 1 block to the other end of each strip set. Carefully check the position of the large triangles to make sure they match the diagram. Make a total of 4 short border strips, 2 of each as shown.

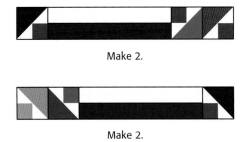

Make 2.

Make 2.

8. Sew a short strip set to the short outer edge of each panel, following the block placement carefully.

← Quilt center

9. Sew the 4 panels together so the border strips are around the outside of the quilt top and the mirror-image panels are side by side, creating the Barn Raising setting.

Quilt Assembly

10. Measure the length of the quilt top through the center; it should be 72½" long. If necessary, trim the outer border strips to fit. Then sew the 72½" outer border strips to the sides of the quilt top. Press the seams toward the outer borders. Likewise, measure the width of the quilt top which should be 73½". Adjust the borders to fit, and then sew the outer border strips to the top and bottom of the quilt top. Press the seams toward the outer borders.

FINISHING

1. Mark the quilt top with a design of your choice.

2. Piece the backing vertically to fit the quilt top.

3. Layer the quilt top with batting and backing; baste.

4. Hand or machine quilt as desired. The quilt shown was machine quilted, with stippling in the light triangles, loops in the inner borders, and a large cable-and-feather design in the outer border.

5. Trim the batting and backing even with the edges of the quilt top. Sew the binding to the quilt.

6. Make a label and attach it to your quilt.

"With All My Heart" detail

▼ ▼ ▼ ▼ ▼ ▼ ▼ ▼ ▼ ▼ ▼ ▼ ▼ ▼ ▼

By Robin Strobel, Issaquah, Washington; quilted by Pam Clarke, Spokane, Washington; 2002.
Finished Quilt Size: 50½" x 56½". Block used: 6" Block A.

Fat-quarter packets of a high-quality flannel in deep, rich colors were the inspiration for this quilt. Normally, I would hesitate to use flannel in this setting because its typically loose weave contributes to the fabric stretching out of shape, and the points can be difficult to match. The flannel I used is all from the same manufacturer and uniformly thick and tightly woven. In addition, the Mary's Triangles construction method decreases the chance of the blocks stretching out of shape. I paid special attention to maintaining a consistent seam allowance, pressed some of the seams open to minimize bulk, and was amazed at how easily the top pieced together.

Using the fabrics interchangeably between the squares and large triangles makes the pinwheels formed by this setting less apparent, while a "butterfly" shape appears. If you want the pinwheels to "pop," use dark-value fabrics for the large and medium-value fabrics for the small squares.

~ Robin Strobel

MATERIALS

Yardage is based on 42"-wide fabric unless otherwise noted.

1½ yds. small floral red print for blocks, border, border corners, and binding

¼ yd. *each* of 6 additional medium-dark red prints for blocks and border

¼ yd. *each* of 7 medium-dark purple prints for blocks and border

¾ yd. beige background fabric for blocks

3½ yds. backing fabric

55" x 61" piece of batting

CUTTING

All measurements include ¼"-wide seam allowances.

From the beige background fabric, cut:
>   4 strips, 4½" x 42"; crosscut into 42 rectangles, 3½" x 4½"

From the 7 assorted red prints, cut a total of:
>   24 squares, 3½" x 3½"
>   10 rectangles, 6" x 7"

From the 7 assorted purple prints, cut a total of:
>   18 squares, 3½" x 3½"
>   11 rectangles, 6" x 7"

From the 6 assorted red prints and the small floral red print, cut:
>   4 squares, 7½" x 7½"
>   6 binding strips, 2½" x 42"

> **Note:** Cutting for the random, scrappy border is detailed in steps 4–6 of "Quilt Top Assembly," opposite.

BLOCK ASSEMBLY

This quilt uses 42 of Block A, which are made in four different color combinations.

1. Sew the red and purple 3½" squares to the ends of the beige 3½" x 4½" rectangles.

2. Sew the pieced strips together in pairs: make 18 pairs with 1 red square and 1 purple square, and make 3 pairs with 2 red squares.

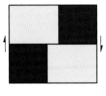 

<table>
<tr><td>Make 18 red and purple.</td><td>Make 3 red and red.</td></tr>
</table>

3. Clip the seam allowances to the seam line between the dark squares. Press the seam away from the dark squares, changing the direction of the seam at the center cut.

4. Pair the units from step 3 with the 6" x 7" red and purple rectangles as follows, and refer to "The Basic Block" on page 5 to mark, sew, and cut the units. Sew red rectangles to 9 of the red/purple units. Sew purple rectangles to the other 9 units. Sew a red rectangle to 1 of the red/red units. Sew purple rectangles to the remaining 2 red/red units. Open the blocks and press the seams toward the dark triangles.

| Purple Triangle, Purple Square Make 9. | Red Triangle, Red Square Make 11. |

| Purple Triangle, Red Square Make 13. | Red Triangle, Purple Square Make 9. |

QUILT TOP ASSEMBLY

1. Arrange the blocks as shown or in an arrangement that is pleasing to you. In the quilt shown, the large triangles in the first 2 rows create alternating purple and red pinwheels. If you look at the pinwheels formed by rows 2 and 3, you will see that they are made from 2 purple and 2 red large triangles. Robin controlled the design of her quilt by placing the large triangles to form the pinwheels and by keeping the squares that meet on the diagonal the same color.

2. Sew the blocks into 7 rows of 6 blocks each, pressing the seams open to reduce bulk. Sew the rows together, once again pressing the seams open.

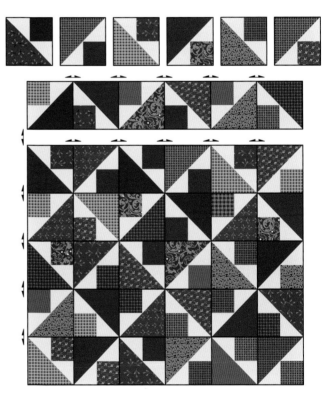

Quilt Assembly

3. Press the quilt top nice and flat. Measure the width and length through the middle, which should be approximately 36½" x 42½". These 2 measurements will be the length of the pieced borders.

RANDOM BORDERS

Cut more wide rectangles than skinny ones because it is less work and does not use up too much fabric. It is difficult to estimate the exact amount of yardage needed for this type of border. If you run out of fabric, the border fabrics do not have to be identical to those in the quilt top. Just use a couple of fat quarters of something that will blend, and your quilt will look terrific.

▲ ▲ ▲ ▲ ▲ ▲ ▲ ▲ ▲ ▲ ▲ ▲ ▲ ▲ ▲ ▲ ▲ ▲ ▲ ▲

4. Cut the red and purple leftovers into random-width rectangles, 1½" to 3½" wide by approximately 8½" long.

5. Sew the long sides of rectangles together until you have a strip the same measurement as the length of the quilt top (approximately 42½"). This will be one of the side borders. Start with one of the widest rectangles at one end and sew randomly until the border is just a little longer than needed. Then you can trim the first wide strip to cut the border to the exact length needed. Trim the border to an even 7½" wide. Repeat for the other side border.

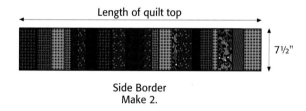

Length of quilt top

7½"

Side Border
Make 2.

6. Sew more rectangles together to make the top and bottom borders. Trim as in step 5 so the borders measure 7½" wide by the width of your quilt top (approximately 36½"). Sew the 7½" medium-dark red squares to each end of the top and bottom borders. Press.

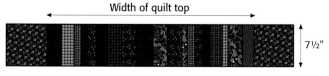

Width of quilt top

7½"

Top and Bottom Border
Make 2.

7. Sew the side borders to the quilt top. Press the seams open to reduce bulk. Sew the top and bottom borders to the quilt top. Press the seams open.

FINISHING

1. Mark the quilt top with a design of your choice.

2. Piece the backing horizontally to fit the quilt top.

3. Layer the quilt top with batting and backing; baste.

4. Hand or machine quilt as desired. The quilt shown was machine quilted with daisylike flowers in the blocks, curved lines in the light areas, and undulating feathers in the pieced borders.

5. Trim the batting and backing even with the edges of the quilt top. Sew the binding to the quilt.

6. Make a label and attach it to your quilt.

MATCHING POINTS

Robin admits that one of the few times she uses pins when making a quilt is when she's trying to match points as she sews rows together. Here's her tip for getting a good match.

1. Align the center seam running between the 2 blocks. Insert a pin directly through the points where the triangles meet.

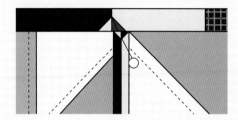

2. Keeping the pin perpendicular to the fabric, insert a second pin to hold the 2 rows together.

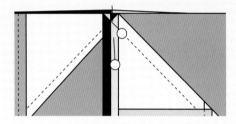

3. Stitch through the visible point. The raw edges may or may not meet cleanly, and your seam allowance may wobble a bit. As long as there is enough fabric in the seam allowance so the seam does not tear out, your quilt will be structurally sound. The wobbles and imperfections usually can be pressed out or will hide nicely after the quilt is quilted.

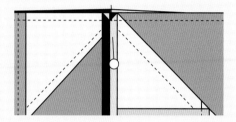

Examine the points after you sew each row. Are they good enough? It depends on your personal tolerance whether or not imperfections need to be resewn. If you decide to resew a mismatched point, rip and stitch only a couple of inches on each side of the recalcitrant seams. Sometimes sewing in the opposite direction (with the bottom fabric on top) will help a stubborn point to line up correctly.

By Margaret E. J. LaBenne, Hendersonville, North Carolina, 2002.
Finished Quilt Size: 58½" x 70½". Block used: 4" Block A. Finished Block Size: 10" x 10".

While the name of the block used in this quilt is "Grandmother's Choice," my group of friends preferred to call it "Sister's Choice" because we felt like sisters, not grandmothers, when we gathered together to work on this quilt project!

Perfect for a little girl's room, soft pastels are just one choice for this quick and easy block. For a boy, how about using bright, bold primary colors? Each finished Grandmother's Choice block consists of four Mary's Triangles blocks, each made of the same fabric. When the Grandmother's Choice blocks are set together with sashing, a secondary Nine Patch pattern emerges. The cornerstones are cut from the same fabrics used in the blocks and are sprinkled randomly through the quilt top to add a touch of sparkle.

~ Marge LaBenne

MATERIALS

Yardage is based on 42"-wide fabric unless otherwise noted.

20 fat eighths (9" x 20") assorted pastel prints for blocks and cornerstones

2¼ yds. white-on-white print for block backgrounds and sashing

2 yds. blue print for border and binding

3¾ yds. backing fabric

63" x 75" piece of batting

CUTTING

All measurements include ¼"-wide seam allowances.

From *each* of the 20 fat eighths, cut:

    2 rectangles, 4½" x 5½" (40 total)

    7 squares, 2½" x 2½" (140 total; 10 are extras)

From the white-on-white print, cut:

    4 strips, 10½" x 42"; crosscut into 49 rectangles, 2½" x 10½"

    5 strips, 4½" x 42"; crosscut into 80 rectangles, 2½" x 4½"

    5 strips, 3½" x 42"; crosscut into 80 rectangles, 2½" x 3½"

From the blue print, cut on the lengthwise grain:

    2 border strips, 4½" x 62½"

    2 border strips, 4½" x 58½"

    4 binding strips, 2½" x 67"

BLOCK ASSEMBLY

Follow the general instructions on page 5 for making Block A. Use the same pastel print for the 2½" squares and for the 4½" x 5½" rectangles in each block. Make 4 of Block A from each pastel for a total of 80 Mary's Triangles blocks.

1. Sew a pastel 2½" square to each of the 2½" x 3½" white rectangles.

2. Sew the pieced strips together into pairs, matching the pastel squares, as shown.

3. Clip the seam allowances to the seam line between the pastel squares. Press the seam allowance away from the pastel squares, changing the direction of the seam at the center cut.

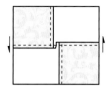

Press seams away
from squares.

4. Pair the units from step 3 with the 4½" x 5½" pastel rectangles of matching fabric, and refer to "The Basic Block" on page 5 to mark, sew, and cut the units. Open the blocks and press the seams toward the pastel triangle.

Make 4 from each fabric
(80 total).

5. Repeat steps 1–4 to make 4 blocks from each pastel fabric for a total of 80 blocks.

6. Lay out 4 matching blocks along with 4 white 2½" x 4½" rectangles and 1 pastel 2½" square as shown.

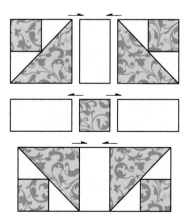

7. Sew the block units together in rows, and then sew the rows together to complete a Grandmother's Choice block. Repeat to make 20 blocks.

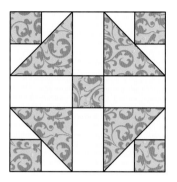

Grandmother's Choice
Make 20.

QUILT TOP ASSEMBLY

1. Sew a 2½" x 10½" white sashing rectangle to one side of each quilt block. Press the seams toward the sashing.

2. Sew the blocks together with the sashing between the blocks. Make 5 rows, each with 4 blocks. Press the seams toward the sashing. Add one sashing rectangle to the end of each row.

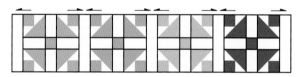

Make 5 rows.

3. Sew a pastel 2½" square to 24 of the 2½" x 10½" white sashing rectangles. Press the seams toward the rectangles.

4. Sew the rectangles into rows, with the cornerstones between the rectangles. Make 6 rows with 4 rectangles each. Add a cornerstone to the end of each row. Press the seams toward the rectangles.

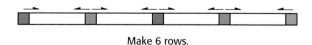

Make 6 rows.

5. Sew the block and sashing rows together to form the quilt top, beginning and ending with the sashing rows. Press the seams toward the sashing.

6. Measure the length of the quilt top through the center; it should measure 62½" long. Adjust the border length to fit if necessary, and then sew the 4½" x 62½" blue border strips to opposite long sides of the quilt top. Press the seams toward the borders. Measure the width of the quilt top through the center; it should be 58½" wide. Adjust the length of the borders if necessary, and then sew the 4½" x 58½" blue borders to the top and bottom of the quilt. Press the seams toward the border strips.

Quilt Assembly

FINISHING

1. Mark the quilt top with a design of your choice.

2. Piece the backing horizontally to fit the quilt top.

3. Layer the quilt top with batting and backing; baste.

4. Hand or machine quilt as desired. The quilt shown was machine quilted in the ditch along the block seams. A cable design was quilted in the border.

5. Trim the batting and backing even with the edges of the quilt top. Sew the binding to the quilt.

6. Make a label and attach it to your quilt.

By Terry Martin, Snohomish, Washington, 2002.
Finished Quilt Size: 25½" x 47¾". Blocks used: 4½" and 9" Block A.

I've been collecting Asian-themed fabric for a while, especially in red, black, and white, and I was planning to use the fabric in a large quilt. When I was invited to make a quilt for *Triangle Tricks* and saw how wonderfully easy it is to make the blocks, I instantly imagined a Japanese-type banner as a quilt. A group of triangles designed on a packing envelope inspired the layout of my quilt. You just never know where inspiration may come from!

~ Terry Martin

MATERIALS

Yardage is based on 42"-wide fabric unless otherwise noted.

⅝ yd. large-scale floral print for blocks and border
⅝ yd. black print for blocks, borders, and binding
⅝ yd. white print for blocks and background
¼ yd. red crane print for blocks
¼ yd. red character print for blocks
1½ yds. backing fabric
30" x 52" piece of batting

CUTTING

All measurements include ¼"-wide seam allowances.

From the large-scale floral print, cut:
    3 rectangles, 9½" x 10½", for the 9" blocks
    1 border strip, 6" x 25½"
From the black print, cut:
    14 squares, 2¾" x 2¾", for the 4½" blocks
    1 border strip, 1½" x 25½"
    1 border strip, 3" x 25½"
    4 binding strips, 2½" x 42"
From the white print, cut:
    6 rectangles, 5" x 6", for the 9" blocks
    14 rectangles, 2¾" x 3¾", for the 4½" blocks
    2 squares, 7¼" x 7¼"; cut once diagonally to yield
        4 corner triangles
    3 squares, 7¾" x 7¾"; cut twice diagonally to
        yield 12 setting triangles

From the red crane print, cut:
    6 squares, 5" x 5", for the 9" blocks
From the red character print, cut:
    7 rectangles, 5" x 6", for the 4½" blocks

BLOCK ASSEMBLY

Follow the general instructions on page 5 for making Block A. You will need six 9" blocks and fourteen 4½" blocks.

1. For the 9" blocks, sew a 5" crane-print square to the ends of the 5" x 6" white rectangles.

2. Sew the pieced strips into pairs as shown.

Make 3.

3. Clip the seam allowances to the seam line between the crane-print squares. Press the seam allowances away from the squares, changing the direction of the seam at the center cut.

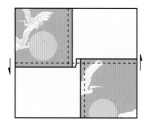

4. Pair the units from step 3 with the 9½" x 10½" floral rectangles, and refer to "The Basic Block" on page 5 to mark, sew, and cut the units. Open the blocks and press the seams toward the floral triangles.

9" Block
Make 6.

5. Repeat steps 2–4 to make fourteen 4½" blocks using the 2¾" black squares, the 2¾" x 3¾" white rectangles, and the 5" x 6" character-print rectangles.

4½" Block
Make 14.

QUILT TOP ASSEMBLY

1. Sew a white setting triangle to the red sides of six 4½" blocks.

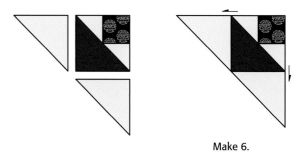

Make 6.

2. Sew the remaining 4½" blocks together in sets of 4 to create 2 large blocks, as shown.

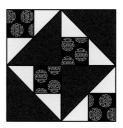

Make 2.

3. Lay out all the blocks and triangle units and sew them into rows as shown.

Quilt Assembly

4. Sew the rows together.

5. Sew the 4 white corner triangles to the corners of the quilt top.

6. Join the 1½" x 25½" black strip and the 6" x 25½" floral strip along their long edges. Sew the strips to the bottom of the quilt top, with the black strip next to the quilt top. Press the seam allowances toward the floral strip.

7. Join the 3" x 25½" black strip to the top of the quilt to complete the quilt top. Press the seam allowance toward the border.

FINISHING

1. Mark the quilt top with a design of your choice.

2. Layer the quilt top with batting and backing; baste the layers together.

3. Hand or machine quilt as desired. The quilt shown was machine quilted using an outline stitch in the small white triangles and around motifs in the floral print, with a crane motif in the corner triangles

4. Trim the batting and backing even with the edges of the quilt top. Sew the binding to the quilt.

5. Make a label and attach it to your quilt.

By Laurie Bevan, Woodinville, Washington; machine quilted by Janet Fogg, Lake Oswego, Oregon; 2002.
Finished Quilt Size: 58" x 70". Blocks used: 2", 4", 6", and 8" Block A.

To challenge myself, I decided to make a quilt combining four different sizes of the Mary's Triangles block. When four blocks of the same size are put together in this pattern, they create a pinwheel, and the pinwheels fit together much like a puzzle. A collection of Provençal fabrics from my stash made a bright and busy palette for this fun quilt—a gift for my husband, Mike, who thinks it's "cool."

~ Laurie Bevan

MATERIALS

All yardages are based on 42"-wide fabric unless otherwise noted.

2 yds. *total* dark prints (reds and blues)

1½ yds. *total* light prints

1¼ yds. *total* medium prints (yellows)

1 yd. blue print for outer border (2 yds. if cutting lengthwise border strips)

¼ yd. yellow print for inner border

3¾ yds. backing fabric

⅝ yd. binding fabric

62" x 74" piece of batting

CUTTING

All measurements include ¼" seam allowances.

From the red dark prints, cut:

    2 rectangles, 8½" x 9½", for the 8" blocks

    4 rectangles, 6½" x 7½", for the 6" blocks

    12 rectangles, 4½" x 5½", for the 4" blocks

    28 rectangles, 2½" x 3½", for the 2" blocks

From the blue dark prints, cut:

    2 rectangles, 8½" x 9½", for the 8" blocks

    8 rectangles, 6½" x 7½", for the 6" blocks

    18 rectangles, 4½" x 5½", for the 4" blocks

    40 rectangles, 2½" x 3½", for the 2" blocks

From the light prints, cut:

    8 rectangles, 4½" x 5½", for the 8" blocks

    24 rectangles, 3½" x 4½", for the 6" blocks

    60 rectangles, 2½" x 3½", for the 4" blocks

    136 rectangles, 1½" x 2½", for the 2" blocks

From the medium prints, cut:

    8 squares, 4½" x 4½", for the 8" blocks

    24 squares, 3½" x 3½", for the 6" blocks

    60 squares, 2½" x 2½", for the 4" blocks

    136 squares, 1½" x 1½", for the 2" blocks

From the yellow print, cut:

    6 inner border strips, 1¼" x 42"

From the blue print, cut:

    6 outer border strips, 4½" x 42", **or**

        if cutting along the lengthwise grain, cut:

        2 strips, 4½" x 62" and 2 strips, 4½" x 58"

From the binding fabric, cut:

    7 strips, 2½" x 42"

BLOCK ASSEMBLY

1. You will need the following numbers of Block A in the sizes indicated. Piece each size set of blocks according to "The Basic Block" on page 5.
   - 8" blocks: make 4 red and 4 blue for two 16" pinwheels
   - 6" blocks: make 8 red and 16 blue for six 12" pinwheels
   - 4" blocks: make 24 red and 36 blue for fifteen 8" pinwheels
   - 2" blocks: make 56 red and 80 blue for thirty-four 4" pinwheels

2. Using 4 blocks of the same size and color, piece a Pinwheel block, taking care to rotate the units as shown. Press the first 2 seams open. This will make

the center points more precise on the finished pinwheel. You can press the final seam to one side.

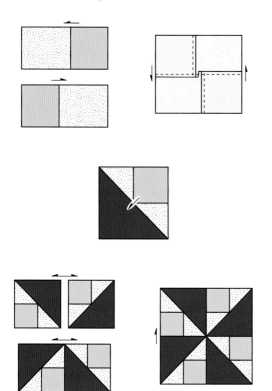

3. Repeat to make all Pinwheel blocks in the sizes specified below.

4"

8"

Make 20 blue.
Make 14 red.

Make 9 blue.
Make 6 red.

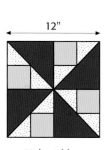

12"

Make 4 blue.
Make 2 red.

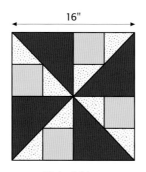

16"

Make 1 blue.
Make 1 red.

QUILT TOP ASSEMBLY

1. Arrange the Pinwheel blocks according to the assembly diagram. Sew the pinwheels together in sections so that you can assemble them into horizontal rows. Then sew the rows together.

Quilt Assembly

2. Measure the length and width of your quilt top. It should be 48½" x 60½". For the inner border, sew three 1¼"-wide strips together. From the long strip, cut a side border 60½" long and a top border 49½" long. Repeat with the remaining three 1¼"-wide strips to cut another side border and the bottom border.

3. Sew the long border strips to opposite sides of the quilt top; press the seams toward the border. Using the short border strips, repeat for the top and bottom borders.

4. For the outer border, if you didn't cut strips from the length of grain, then sew three 4½"-wide strips together. From the long strip, cut a side border 62" long and a top border 58" long. Repeat with the remaining three 4½"-wide strips to cut another side border and the bottom border.

5. Sew the long border strips to opposite sides of the quilt top; press the seams toward the outer border. Using the short border strips, repeat for the top and bottom borders.

FINISHING

1. Mark the quilt top with a design of your choice.

2. Piece the backing horizontally to fit the quilt top.

3. Layer the quilt top with batting and backing; baste.

4. Hand or machine quilt as desired. The quilt shown was machine quilted with a swirling pattern to simulate pinwheels blowing in the breeze.

5. Trim the batting and backing even with the edges of the quilt top. Sew the binding to the quilt.

6. Make a label and attach it to your quilt.

DIAMOND MAZE

▼▼▼▼▼▼▼▼▼▼▼▼▼▼▼▼▼▼

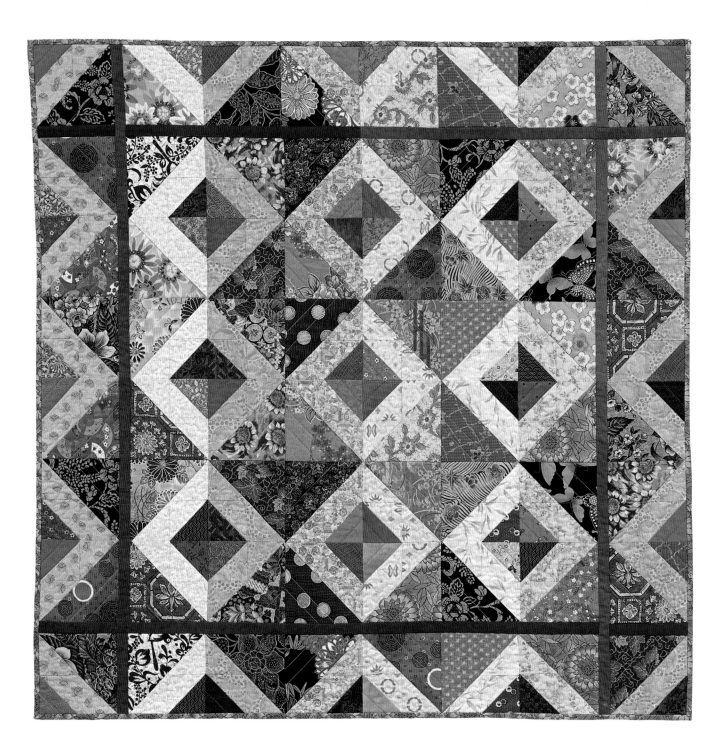

By Ellen Pahl, Coopersburg, Pennsylvania, 2002.
Finished Quilt Size: 42" x 42". Block used: 5" Block B.

Dig into your fabric stash to make a scrappy quilt from a variation of the Mary's Triangles block. The placement of lights and darks in the small triangle square have been reversed in the block, and in this setting that gives the illusion of a maze, zigzagging back and forth. The larger portion of the blocks are great for showcasing some of your favorite fabrics, such as the Japanese fabrics used in the quilt shown. Use small-scale prints or solids in the smaller, dark triangle portion of the block.

~ Ellen Pahl

MATERIALS

All yardages are based on 42"-wide fabric unless otherwise noted.

1½ yds. *total* of 12 to 16 medium to dark large-scale prints for large triangles

½ yd. *total* of 9 medium to dark solids for narrow accent border

¼ yd. or fat quarter *each* of 8 light prints for background

Scraps or ½ yd. *total* of 12 to 16 medium to dark small-scale prints for small triangles

2 yds. backing fabric

½ yd. binding fabric

46" x 46" piece of batting

CUTTING

All measurements include ¼" seam allowances.

From *each* of the 8 light prints, cut:
 4 squares, 3⅜" x 3⅜"
 8 rectangles, 3" x 4"

From the medium to dark small-scale prints, cut:
 32 squares, 3⅜" x 3⅜"

From the medium to dark large-scale prints, cut:
 32 rectangles, 5½" x 6½"

From the medium to dark solids, cut:
 3 strips, 1¼" x 21¼"
 1 strip, 1¼" x 20½"
 1 strip, 1¼" x 16¼"
 2 strips, 1¼" x 15½"
 1 strip, 1¼" x 10½"
 5 strips, 1¼" x 5½"

From the binding fabric, cut:
 5 strips, 2½" x 42"

BLOCK ASSEMBLY

Work with one background fabric at a time to make the 8 blocks for each row.

1. Layer a 3⅜" light square with a medium print 3⅜" square, right sides together. Draw a line diagonally from corner to corner on the wrong side of the light square.

2. Stitch ¼" away from the drawn line on both sides. Cut apart on the drawn line to create 2 triangle squares. Press the seams toward the darker fabric.

EASY MARKING

The Quick Quarter II, available at quilt shops, is a great little tool for marking diagonally across squares. You can mark the center diagonal line and/or the stitching lines quickly and accurately with it.

To avoid marking entirely, you can use another tool, available at quilt shops, called The Angler. Tape this plastic grid to the bed of your sewing machine, following the package directions, and then guide your squares along the marked lines on The Angler for accurate sewing with no marking.

3. Sew a triangle square to each corresponding 3" x 4" light rectangle as shown. Press.

4. Sew pairs of these units together as shown. The triangles in this quilt were mixed and matched so that the 2 resulting blocks did not have the same fabric used for the small triangles. The dark triangles should be on the outer corners of the unit. Clip the seam allowance to the seam line in the center so that you can press seams away from the triangle-square units.

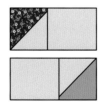

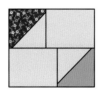

5. Pair the units from step 4 with the 5½" x 6½" medium and dark rectangles, and refer to the "The Basic Block" on page 5 to mark, sew, and cut the units. You will make 8 blocks from each background fabric for a total of 64 blocks. You may want to wait until after you arrange your blocks before pressing the diagonal seam so that you can press seams in adjoining blocks in opposite directions for easier assembly.

Make 8 of each background
(64 total).

QUILT TOP ASSEMBLY

1. Arrange the blocks and accent border as shown in the assembly diagram. The 8 blocks of each background should create 1 vertical row. Rearrange your blocks until you are pleased with the overall look of your quilt. Press the diagonal seams of the blocks in opposite directions from block to block.

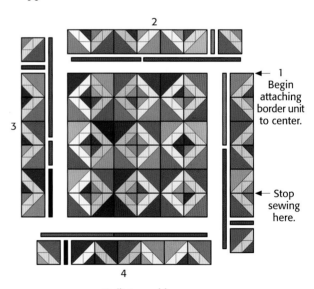

Quilt Assembly

2. Piece the accent border strips as shown in the quilt assembly diagram above. Border seams should be pressed in the opposite direction from the neighboring blocks.

3. Sew the 6 rows of 6 blocks together for the quilt center. Press the seams in opposite directions from row to row. Sew the border blocks together into 2 horizontal and 2 vertical rows.

4. Join the border blocks with the accent border strips as shown in the assembly diagram to create 4 border units.

5. Add the border units one at a time, using a partial-seam technique for the first border. Refer to the assembly diagram, opposite. Start at one corner and pin the border unit to the quilt center. Sew the seam until you reach the last block. Stop stitching and remove the quilt from the sewing machine.

6. Attach the next border unit, again referring to the assembly diagram for the sewing order. You will be able to sew the complete border seam if you rotate your quilt in a clockwise manner and attach the border units in that sequence.

7. After adding the last border unit, you can go back to the first border unit and complete the seam.

FINISHING

1. Mark the quilt top with a design of your choice.

2. Piece the backing vertically to fit the quilt top.

3. Layer the quilt top with batting and backing; baste.

4. Hand or machine quilt as desired. The quilt shown was machine quilted with meandering in the light fabrics, and straight parallel lines in the large and small squares formed where the dark triangles meet.

5. Trim the batting and backing even with the edges of the quilt top. Sew the binding to the quilt.

6. Make a label and attach it to your quilt.

By Barbara J. Eikmeier, Carlisle, Pennsylvania, 2002.
Finished Quilt Size: 59½" x 75½". Block used: 4" Block B. Finished Block Size: 16" x 16".

What a charming way to make a scrap quilt! Whether you love the look of the 1930s style prints, or thoroughly modern suits your taste, Pinwheel Star blocks are a great way to showcase both your fabrics and the Mary's Triangles technique. What's amazing is that the triangle units seem to disappear and the stars become the focus. In this setting, the blocks are set right next to one another, without sashing or alternate blocks. This plan creates large, plain areas where your quilting will set off the individual stars.

~ Barb Eikmeier

MATERIALS

All yardages are based on 42"-wide fabric unless otherwise noted.

2 yds. muslin for block backgrounds
1 yd. yellow print for outer border
½ yd. blue print for inner border
¼ yd. *each* of 6 assorted solids for pinwheels
¼ yd. *each* of 12 assorted medium prints for stars
⅛ yd. *each* of 6 assorted light prints for stars
4 yds. backing fabric
⅝ yd. binding fabric
64" x 80" piece of batting

CUTTING

All measurements include ¼" seam allowances.

From the muslin, cut:
    6 strips, 4½" x 42"; crosscut into 48 squares, 4½" x 4½"
    6 strips, 5½" x 42"; crosscut into 48 rectangles, 4½" x 5½"

From *each* of the assorted solids, cut:
    4 rectangles, 4½" x 5½" (you need 2 matching rectangles per block)

From *each* of the medium prints, cut:
    1 strip, 3½" x 42"; crosscut into 12 rectangles, 2½" x 3½" (144 total)
    1 strip, 2⅞" x 42"; crosscut into 6 squares, 2⅞" x 2⅞" (72 total)

From *each* of the light prints, cut:
    1 strip, 2⅞" x 42"; crosscut into 12 squares, 2⅞" x 2⅞" (72 total)

From the blue print, cut:
    6 inner border strips, 2" x 42"

From the yellow print, cut:
    7 outer border strips, 4½" x 42"

From the binding fabric, cut:
    7 strips, 2½" x 42"

BLOCK ASSEMBLY

The instructions are for making one Pinwheel Star block at a time. For each block, gather 4 muslin 4½" squares, 4 muslin 4½" x 5½" rectangles, 2 matching solid 4½" x 5½" rectangles, 12 matching medium print 2½" x 3½" rectangles, 6 matching medium print 2⅞" squares, and 6 matching light print 2⅞" squares.

1. On the wrong side of the 2⅞" light print squares, draw a diagonal line from corner to corner. Place the squares right sides together with the 2⅞" medium print squares. Stitch ¼" away from the drawn lines on both sides. Cut apart on the lines to create 2 triangle squares. Press the seams toward the medium print triangles.

Make 12.

2. Sew a triangle square to each corresponding 2½" x 3½" rectangle as shown. Press the seams toward the rectangles. Make 12 matching units.

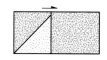

Make 12.

3. Sew pairs of the units from step 2 together as shown. Clip the seam allowance to the seam line in the center so that you can press the seams away from the triangle squares. Make 6.

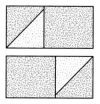

Make 6.

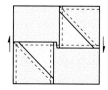

4. Pair the units from step 3 with the 4½" x 5½" rectangles. Make 4 with muslin rectangles and the other 2 with solid rectangles, which will result in 4 blocks with large solid rectangles and 8 blocks with large muslin triangles. Refer to the "The Basic Block" on page 5 to mark, sew, and cut the units. Press the seams toward the solid fabric. On the muslin units, press half of the seams *toward* the muslin and the other half *away from* the muslin to make it easier to assemble the star block.

Make 4.   Make 4.   Make 4.

5. For the top and bottom rows of the star block, arrange and sew the units into rows as shown. In each row, use 1 unit with the seam pressed toward the muslin and 1 with the seam pressed away from the muslin so the adjoining seams fall in alternating directions. Press the seams in the row to the left. Make 2 of these rows.

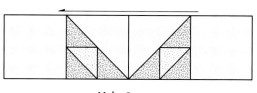

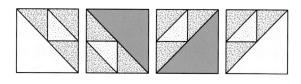

Make 2 rows.

6. For the 2 center rows, arrange and sew the units into rows as shown. Match and pin the points of the small triangles where they meet. Use a unit with the seam pressed toward the muslin on one end and a unit with the seam pressed away from the muslin on the other end. Press the seams to the right. Make 2.

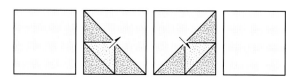

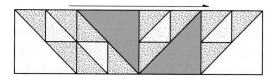

Make 2 rows.

7. Arrange and sew the rows into a block. Press the seams in one direction. Repeat to make a total of 12 Pinwheel Star blocks.

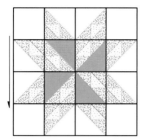

Pinwheel Star Block
Make 12.

QUILT TOP ASSEMBLY

1. Arrange the blocks in 4 rows of 3 blocks each. When laying out the blocks, pay attention to the direction of the seam allowances. If the seams are pressed in the same direction, rotate the block so they go in alternate directions. It is easiest to first decide on the color placement, and then rotate the blocks, beginning in a corner and working in rows across the quilt.

2. Sew the blocks into rows and number them. Press the seams in the odd-numbered rows toward the left, and press the seams in the even-numbered rows toward the right. Sew the rows together. Press the seams in one direction.

3. Sew 3 blue border strips together, end to end. Repeat with the other 3 strips. Measure the quilt top through the center from side to side. From each of the long strips, cut a border to this measurement, which should be approximately 48½" long. Sew the borders to the top and bottom of the quilt; press the seams toward the border.

4. Measure the quilt top through the center from top to bottom. From the remaining blue strips, cut 2 border strips to this measurement, which should be approximately 67½". Sew them to the sides of the quilt and press as for the top and bottom borders.

5. Make the yellow outer border in the same manner as the inner blue border, sewing the border strips together in sets and trimming them to the width and length of your quilt. For the top and bottom borders, sew 3 yellow strips together and cut 2 border strips from the long strip (approximately 51½" long). For the side borders, sew the remaining 4 strips together in pairs. From each long strip, cut 1 border strip to fit the sides of the quilt (approximately 75½" long).

Quilt Assembly

FINISHING

1. Mark the quilt top with a design of your choice.

2. Piece the backing horizontally to fit the quilt top.

3. Layer the quilt top with batting and backing; baste.

4. Hand or machine quilt as desired. The quilt shown was machine quilted with hearts and feathers in the light areas and continuous swirls in the borders.

5. Trim the batting and backing even with the edges of the quilt top. Sew the binding to the quilt.

6. Make a label and attach it to your quilt.

By Sally Schneider, Albuquerque, New Mexico, 2002.
Finished Quilt Size: 44½" x 52½". Blocks used: 4" Block A and 4" Block B.

Of all the ways to put triangles together, my favorite designs are stars. And that's just where I started with this quilt. For the interesting medallion-type star center, I made Mary's Triangles using the pinwheel variation. To set off the star, a ring of blocks made with plain squares came next. The outer borders are pieced from Mary's Triangles blocks made with triangle squares. This combination of all the block options makes for a dynamic setting, one where the Mary's Triangles block is really the star.

~ Sally Schneider

MATERIALS

All yardages are based on 42"-wide fabric unless otherwise noted.

2 yds. *total* assorted dark prints (include scrap of blue and scrap of gold for star center) for blocks

1½ yds. light blue print for background

½ yd. red print for star points and inner border

3 yds. backing fabric

½ yd. binding fabric

50" x 58" piece of batting

CUTTING

All measurements include ¼" seam allowances.

From the light blue print, cut:
  8 strips, 3½" x 42"; crosscut into 128 rectangles, 2½" x 3½"
  4 strips, 2⅞" x 42"; crosscut into 50 squares, 2⅞" x 2⅞"

From the assorted dark prints, cut:
  50 squares, 2⅞" x 2⅞"
  24 squares, 2½" x 2½"
  58 rectangles, 4½" x 5½"

From the red print, cut:
  1 strip, 4½" x 42"; crosscut into 4 rectangles, 4½" x 5½"; from the remainder of the strip, cut 2 squares, 2⅞" x 2⅞"
  4 border strips, 2½" x 42"

From the gold scrap, cut:
  2 squares, 2⅞" x 2⅞"

From the blue scrap, cut:
  2 rectangles, 4½" x 5½"

From the binding fabric, cut:
  6 strips, 2½" x 42"

BLOCK ASSEMBLY

1. Draw a line diagonally from corner to corner on the wrong side of the 2⅞" light blue squares. Layer these squares with the 2⅞" assorted dark squares, right sides together.

2. Stitch ¼" away from the drawn line on both sides. Cut apart on the drawn line to create 2 triangle squares. Press the seam toward the dark fabric. Make a total of 100 triangle squares that are half light blue, half dark print.

Make 100 assorted.

3. Repeat steps 1 and 2, using 2 red 2⅞" squares and 2 gold 2⅞" squares to yield 4 half-red, half-gold triangle squares.

Make 4.

4. For the 5 pinwheels in the center of the quilt, choose 5 groups of 4 matching triangle squares. One group will be the red and gold triangle squares made in step 3. Sew each triangle square to a 2½" x 3½" light blue rectangle, taking care to arrange the colors as shown, or the pinwheels won't appear.

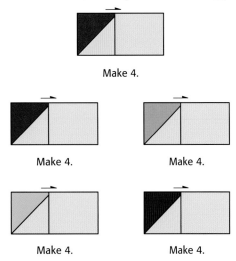

Make 4.

Make 4.   Make 4.

Make 4.   Make 4.

5. Sew pairs of these units together, making 2 pairs of the center pinwheel color and 1 pair with each of the remaining 4 colors.

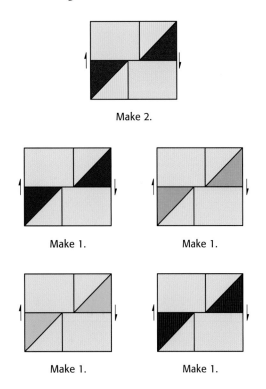

Make 2.

Make 1.   Make 1.

Make 1.   Make 1.

6. Sew the remaining triangle-square/rectangle units together in pairs, but this time mix up the color combinations. That way, each pinwheel color will be sewn to a different color rectangle to keep things scrappy.

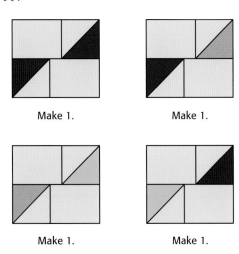

Make 1.   Make 1.

Make 1.   Make 1.

7. To make the center red-and-gold pinwheel, place the units with the red-and-gold triangle squares right sides together with 4½" x 5½" blue rectangles. (You can use another color if you like, but both rectangles should be from the same fabric.) Refer to the "The Basic Block" on page 5 to mark, sew, and cut the units. Reserve these completed blocks for the center of the star.

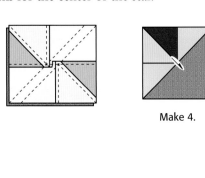

Make 4.

8. Place each of the 4 *matching* triangle-square/rectangle units together with a 4½" x 5½" red rectangle. Mark, sew, and cut the units.

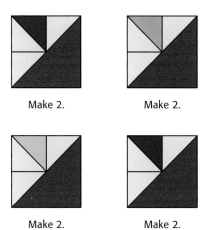

Make 2.   Make 2.

Make 2.   Make 2.

9. Place the remaining 4 triangle-square units (the ones with 2 different-color triangle squares) together with assorted 4½" x 5½" rectangles. Mark, sew, and cut as before. Reserve these units to complete the pinwheels around the center star.

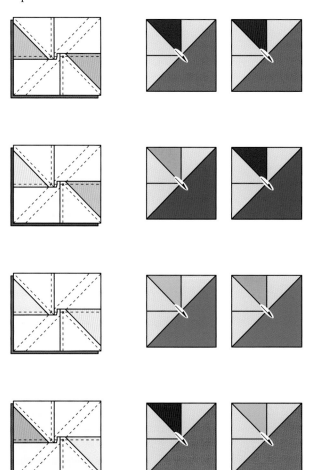

10. Sew all of the remaining triangle squares to 2½" x 3½" light blue rectangles as shown. Sew the units together in pairs, mixing up the colors. Pair these units with assorted 4½" x 5½" rectangles and mark, sew, and cut the units as you did in step 8. These B blocks will be used for the pieced outer border.

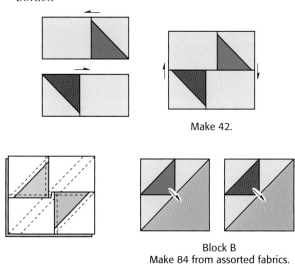

Make 42.

Block B
Make 84 from assorted fabrics.

11. Sew the 2½" dark squares to the remainder of the 2½" x 3½" light blue rectangles. Sew the square/rectangle units together in pairs, mixing up the colors. Pair these units with assorted 4½" x 5½" rectangles and mark, sew, and cut the units as you did in step 8. These A blocks will be used to surround the star in the center of the quilt.

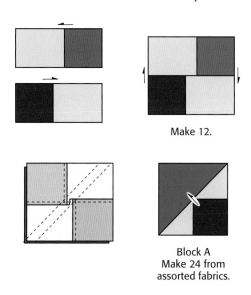

Make 12.

Block A
Make 24 from assorted fabrics.

SIZE IT UP!

This quilt, with its central medallion, would look terrific on a bed if it were sized to fit. It's easy enough to enlarge the quilt by simply making larger blocks, not more blocks. Instead of the 4" blocks that Sally used, make 7" blocks for a twin-size quilt or 9" blocks for a queen-size quilt.

Yardage requirements for these sizes are given below. For cutting, you'll need to cut the same number of pieces as given in the cutting list for the project, but refer to the cutting charts on pages 10 and 11 to determine what size of squares and rectangles to cut.

Fabric	Twin	Queen
	74" x 88"	94" x 108"
Light blue for background	2¾ yds.	4½ yds.
Red print for stars and inner border	¾ yd.	1¼ yds.
Assorted dark prints	4½ yds.	7 yds.
Backing fabric	5⅜ yds.	8⅝ yds.
Binding fabric	¾ yd.	⅞ yd.
Batting	78" x 92"	98" x 112"

QUILT TOP ASSEMBLY

1. Gather the Mary's Triangles units completed in steps 6–9 of "Block Assembly" on pages 48–49 for the star center of the quilt.

2. Arrange the red star points, the blue center units, and 4 multicolored units as shown. Sew them together in rows; sew the rows together.

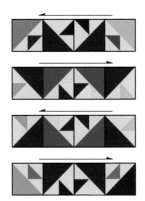 

3. Arrange the reserved blocks from step 7 of "Block Assembly" to complete the pinwheels around the center star as shown. Add the A blocks (with squares in the corners) to complete the quilt center. Sew the blocks together in rows, and then sew the rows together.

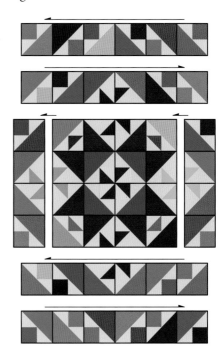

4. Measure the length of the quilt top and trim 2 of the 2½" x 42" red border strips to this length, which should be approximately 32½". Sew a strip to each side of the quilt. Press the seams toward the borders.

5. Measure the width of the quilt top and trim the 2 remaining red border strips to this length, which should be approximately 28½". Sew the border strips to the top and bottom of the quilt top. Press the seams toward the border.

6. Arrange 18 B blocks (with triangle corners) as shown for each of the side borders. Sew the blocks together.

Side Border
Make 2.

7. Sew the pieced borders to the sides of the quilt top, arranging them as shown, and press the seams toward the red border.

8. Arrange 22 B blocks as shown for each of the top and bottom borders. Sew the blocks together, and then add the borders to the top and bottom edges of the quilt top, referring to the quilt photograph on page 46 for placement.

Top and Bottom Border
Make 2.

QUILT FINISHING

1. Mark the quilt top with a design of your choice.

2. Piece the backing horizontally to fit the quilt top.

3. Layer the quilt top with batting and backing; baste.

4. Hand or machine quilt as desired. The quilt shown was machine quilted with sets of straight, parallel lines in the dark areas and looping lines in the chain of squares.

5. Trim the batting and backing even with the edges of the quilt top. Sew the binding to the quilt.

6. Make a label and attach it to your quilt.

By Laurie Bevan, Woodinville, Washington; machine quilted by Pam Clarke, Spokane, Washington; 2002.
Finished Quilt Size: 72½" x 90½". Block used: 9" Block B.

We lose power quite often at our beach house on the Kitsap Peninsula in Washington State, so I want to have lots of warm and cozy quilts to pile on the beds on those cold, heatless nights. That's why I chose flannel fabric for "Winter Comfort." While flannel can be tricky to work with when stitching lots of tiny, bias-edge pieces, it was easy to make the large 9" blocks using the Mary's Triangles technique. This bed-size quilt went together quickly, and I know I'll be snuggling under its warmth for many winters to come.

~ Laurie Bevan

MATERIALS

Yardage is based on 42"-wide fabric unless otherwise noted.

3¼ yds. *total* assorted dark prints

3 yds. *total* assorted light prints

1 yd. *total* assorted medium prints

5¾ yds. backing fabric

¾ yd. binding fabric

77" x 95" piece of batting

CUTTING

All measurements include ¼" seam allowances.

From the assorted light prints, cut:

    80 rectangles, 5" x 6"

    40 squares, 5⅜" x 5⅜"

From the assorted medium prints; cut:

    40 squares, 5⅜" x 5⅜"

From the assorted dark prints, cut:

    40 rectangles, 9½" x 10½"

From the binding fabric, cut:

    9 strips, 2½" x 42"

BLOCK ASSEMBLY

You need 80 triangle squares with an unfinished size of 5". Use your favorite method for creating the triangle squares or follow the directions in step 1 below to make the triangle squares.

1. Choose 1 light print and 1 medium print 5⅜" square. Draw a diagonal line on the wrong side of the light square. Place it right sides together with the medium square. Stitch ¼" away from each side of the line. Cut apart on the line to create 2 triangle squares. Press the seams toward the medium print triangles. Repeat, pairing each of the 40 light squares with a medium print square to make a total of 80 triangle squares.

2. Sew the triangle squares to the light print 5" x 6" rectangles as shown. Press the seams toward the rectangles.

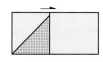

Make 80.

3. Sew pairs of the units from step 2 together as shown. Clip the seam allowances to the seam line in the center so that you can press seams away from the triangle squares. Make 40.

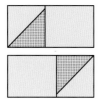 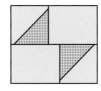

Make 40.

4. Pair the units from step 3 with the 9½" x 10½" dark print rectangles. Refer to the "The Basic Block" on page 5 to mark, sew, and cut the units. Press the seams toward the large triangles.

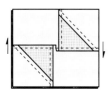

Make 80.

QUILT TOP ASSEMBLY

1. Arrange the blocks according to the quilt assembly diagram to create the Barn Raising setting.

Quilt Assembly

2. Sew the blocks together into rows. Press the seam allowances in opposite directions from row to row for easier assembly.

3. Sew the rows together. Press the quilt top.

FINISHING

1. Mark the quilt top with a design of your choice.

2. Piece the backing vertically to fit the quilt top.

3. Layer the quilt top with batting and backing; baste.

4. Hand or machine quilt as desired. The quilt shown was machine quilted with feather motifs in the dark bands and with free-form vines and flowers in the light bands.

5. Trim the batting and backing even with the edges of the quilt top. Sew the binding to the quilt.

6. Make a label and attach it to your quilt.

By Sally Schneider, Albuquerque, New Mexico; machine quilted by Kari Lane, Lansing, Kansas; 2002.
Finished Quilt Size: 58½" x 74½". Block used: 8" Kansas Troubles.

At first glance this quilt may look nothing like the other quilts in this book. But I've adapted my original triangle technique to use in different circumstances, such as with the Kansas Troubles blocks in this quilt. The block only looks complex. It's not hard to piece, especially when you adapt the Mary's Triangles shortcut technique to its construction. Many traditional patterns are divided in half diagonally like this one, and you can assemble any of them using the Mary's Triangle technique.

~ Sally Schneider

MATERIALS

Yardage is based on 42"-wide fabric unless otherwise noted.

3 yds. *total* of assorted dark prints for blocks

1⅝ yds. blue print for outer border and binding

1 yd. *total* of assorted light prints for blocks

½ yd. brown print for inner border

3½ yds. backing fabric

62" x 78" piece of batting

CUTTING

All measurements include ¼"-wide seam allowances.

From the assorted dark prints, cut:

    6 strips, 8½" x 42"; crosscut into 24 rectangles, 8½" x 9½"

    3 strips, 3½" x 42"; crosscut into 48 rectangles, 2½" x 3½"

    3 strips, 5½" x 42"; crosscut into 24 rectangles, 4½" x 5½"

    8 strips, 2⅞" x 42"; crosscut into 96 squares, 2⅞" x 2⅞"

From the assorted light prints, cut:

    3 strips, 2½" x 42"; crosscut into 48 squares, 2½" x 2½"

    8 strips, 2⅞" x 42"; crosscut into 96 squares, 2⅞" x 2⅞"

From the brown print, cut:

    8 border strips, 1½" x 42"

From the blue print, cut:

    8 border strips, 4½" x 42"

    8 binding strips, 2½" x 42"

BLOCK ASSEMBLY

1. Layer a 2⅞" light square with a 2⅞"dark square, right sides together. Draw a line diagonally from corner to corner on the wrong side of the light square.

2. Stitch ¼" from the drawn line on both sides. Cut apart on the drawn line to create 2 triangle squares. Press the seams toward the darker fabric. Repeat, using all of the 2⅞" light and dark squares. You'll have a total of 192 light-and-dark triangle squares.

Make 192.

3. Sew pairs of bias squares together. Be sure the dark and light triangles face the proper direction. You'll need 48 pairs to face one way, and 48 pairs to face the opposite direction.

Make 48.   Make 48.

4. To the pairs with dark fabric in the bottom left corners, add 2½" light squares to the left end and 2½" x 3½" dark rectangles to the right ends, as shown.

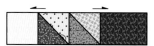

Make 48.

5. Sew the remaining pairs to the short sides of the 4½" x 5½" dark rectangles. Be sure to orient them as shown.

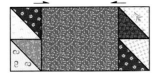

Make 24.

6. Add the units from step 4 to the units from step 5, as shown. Clip the seam allowance in the space between the rectangle squares, just as you would for a regular Mary's Triangle unit. Press the seams away from the triangle squares, changing the direction of the seam at the center cut.

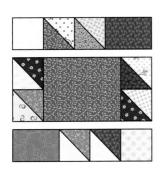

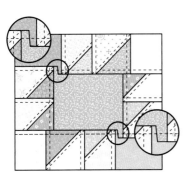

7. Layer each unit, right sides together, with an 8½" x 9½" dark rectangle, referring to "The Basic Block" on page 5 to mark, sew, and cut the units. Press the seam allowances toward the resulting large dark triangles.

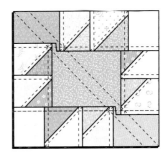

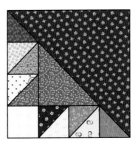

Make 48.

QUILT TOP ASSEMBLY

1. Arrange the blocks in rows as shown. Make a total of 8 rows.

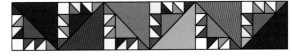

Make 8.

2. Sew the rows together, alternating the direction from one row to the next so your quilt looks like that shown.

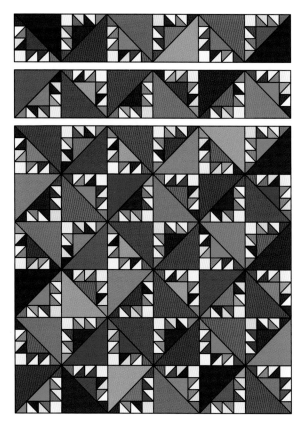

Quilt Assembly

3. Sew the 1½"-wide brown strips end to end in pairs. Measure the quilt top through the center from top to bottom. From 2 of the long strips, cut a border to this measurement, which should be approximately 64½" long. Sew the borders to the sides of the quilt top, pressing the seams toward the border.

4. Measure the quilt top from side to side. From the remaining brown strips, cut 2 borders to this length, which should be approximately 50½". Sew the borders to the top and bottom of the quilt and press as for the side borders.

5. Make the outer borders in the same manner as for the inner border, sewing the blue strips together in pairs and trimming them to the length and width of your quilt. The side borders should be approximately 66½" long, and the top and bottom borders should be approximately 58½" long.

FINISHING

1. Mark the quilt top with a design of your choice.

2. Piece the backing horizontally to fit the quilt top.

3. Layer the quilt top with batting and backing; baste.

4. Hand or machine quilt as desired. The quilt shown was quilted with a grid pattern over the blocks, and with a vine and leaf pattern in the outer border.

5. Trim the batting and backing even with the edges of the quilt top. Sew the binding to the quilt.

6. Make a label and attach it to your quilt.

QUILT GALLERY

Cosmic Double X by Cornelia Heitz Gauger, Everett, Washington, 2002. Block used: 6" Block A.

Cornelia, who is a self-professed "queen of celestial fabrics," thought it would be fun to make a wall hanging out of her collection. "I found the idea for the Double X layout in *Designing Quilts: The Value of Value* (That Patchwork Place, 1994) and saw the potential for modifying it to form a star pattern. I used background squares in the corners instead of the Shaded Four Patch to give the design a star shape."

Whale Tales by Margaret Schmidt, Monroe, Washington;
quilted by Rhoda Lonergan; 2002. Block used: 5" Block A.
Notice how Margaret used the same blue solid fabric for the large triangles as she did for the borders.
Her color placement gives the smaller pieces of whale fabric more prominence. When
Margaret found the whale fabric, she said, "It cried out to be in a quilt!"

Tropical Gems by Leanne Clare, Everett, Washington, 1998. Block used: 4½" Block A.
Leanne confesses that she was enchanted with the possibilities she saw in Suzanne Hammond's book
Designing Quilts: The Value of Value (That Patchwork Place, 1994). Using her favorite colors,
Leanne sewed for four solid days to construct this "retreat project."

Wildflowers by Virginia Lauth, Shoreline, Washington, 2002. Block used: 3" Block A.
Virginia decided to set her triangle blocks on point and used scrappy fabrics to give the illusion of a
garden of wildflowers. She adds, "I have used scraps ranging from childhood dresses to
the latest prints in the quilt shops to give the quilt a wide range of color."

It's Bright, Baby by Rhoda Lonergan, Monroe, Washington, 2002.

Block used: 5" Block A.

Rhoda thought it would be fun to use some bright fabric she had on hand to make Mary's Triangles blocks. The quilt gets its name from the whimsical lightbulb fabric used in the quilt.

Starburst Fruit Chews by Suzanne Kolhagen, North Charleston, South Carolina, 2002. Block used: 5" Block A. Suzanne started making the block units with the idea of creating vines with flower buds, but when arranging and rearranging her blocks, she liked this combination best, even though it was totally different from her original plan. Her son, Jeff, came up with the name. "When he passed by my sewing room and noticed the block arrangement on the floor, Jeff stopped and said, 'That's cool, Mom. It looks just like Starburst Fruit Chews!'"

Oh, Those Batiks! by Rhoda Lonergan, Monroe, Washington, 2002.
Blocks used: 8" Block A and 4" Block A.

According to Rhoda, her stash of batiks was getting mighty big and she was trying
to use them up. "My husband really likes this quilt, so now it is his."

Secondhand Fish by Leanne Clare, Everett, Washington, 2001. Block used: 7½" Block B.
Leanne had an extensive collection of fabrics from the 1950s and 1960s, all obtained at garage sales, rummage sales, or secondhand stores. She used the fabrics to make large Mary's Triangles blocks so she could showcase each funky fabric individually. Leanne exclaims, "Every single piece of fabric used in this quilt is secondhand!"

Roundabout by Stan Green, Monroe, Washington; quilted by Barbara Dau; 2002. Block used: 4" Block A.
The inspiration for "Roundabout" came from traditional Amish quilts. Stan started out with a Jacob's Ladder block and reworked the components into this original quilt design. The Amish theme is carried through in the quilting, too, with undulating feathers filling the wide outer border.

Christmas Star by Karen Costello Soltys, Monroe, Washington, 2002. Block used: 5" Block A.
While looking for an interesting block to showcase a favorite print fabric, Karen discovered the traditional
Christmas Star block. She says, "The piecing looked complicated, but by substituting Mary's Triangles
blocks for many of the individual triangle pieces, the block was much easier to assemble accurately."

One for the Boys by Nicki McAuliffe, Snohomish, Washington;
quilted by Rhoda Lonergan; 2002. Block used: 8" Block A.
Nicki named this quilt for her husband and son.
She let them choose the colors so they'd enjoy curling up with it.

QUILTMAKING BASICS

▼ ▼

Whether you're new to quiltmaking or you're simply ready to learn a new technique, you'll find this quiltmaking basics section filled with information that can help you make any of the projects in this book. Read through it now, or refer to it as needed for help with piecing, attaching borders, or finding the right tool for the job.

FABRICS AND SUPPLIES

Fabrics: Select high-quality, 100 percent–cotton fabrics. They hold their shape well and are easy to handle.

Sewing machine: To machine piece, you'll need a sewing machine that has a good straight stitch. You'll also need a walking foot or darning foot if you are going to machine quilt.

Rotary-cutting tools: You will need a rotary cutter, a cutting mat, and a clear acrylic ruler. Rotary-cutting rulers are available in a variety of sizes; some of the most frequently used sizes include 6" x 6", 6" x 12", 6" x 24", and 12" x 12" or 15" x 15".

Thread: Use a good-quality, all-purpose cotton or cotton-covered polyester thread.

Needles: For machine piecing, a size 10/70 or 12/80 works well for most cottons. For machine quilting, a larger-size needle, such as a 14/90, works best. For hand quilting, use "betweens," which are short, very sharp needles made specifically for this purpose.

Pins: Long, fine silk pins (with or without glass heads) slip easily through fabric, making them perfect for patchwork.

Scissors: Use your best scissors for cutting fabric only. Sharp embroidery scissors or thread snips are handy for clipping threads.

Template plastic: Use clear or frosted plastic (available at quilt shops) to make durable, accurate templates.

Seam ripper: Use this tool to remove stitches from incorrectly sewn seams.

Marking tools: A variety of tools are available to mark fabric when tracing around templates or marking quilting designs. Use a sharp No. 2 pencil or a fine-lead mechanical pencil on lighter-colored fabrics, and use a silver or chalk pencil on darker fabrics. Chalk pencils or chalk-wheel markers make clear marks on fabric and are easier to remove than grease-based colored pencils. Always test your marking tool to make sure you can remove the marks easily.

ROTARY CUTTING

Instructions for quick-and-easy rotary cutting are provided wherever possible. All measurements include standard ¼"-wide seam allowances. If you are unfamiliar with rotary cutting, read the brief introduction that follows. For more detailed information, see *Shortcuts: A Concise Guide to Rotary Cutting* by Donna Lynn Thomas (Martingale & Company, 1999).

1. Fold the fabric and match selvages, aligning the crosswise and lengthwise grains as much as possible. Place the folded edge closest to you on the cutting mat. Align a square ruler such as a Bias Square along the folded edge of the fabric. Place a long, straight ruler to the left of the square ruler, just covering the uneven raw edges on the left side of the fabric.

2. Remove the square ruler and cut along the right edge of the long ruler, rolling the rotary cutter away

from you. Discard this strip. (Reverse this procedure if you are left-handed.)

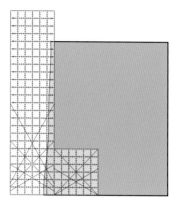

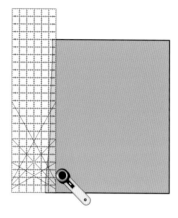

3. To cut strips, align the newly cut edge of the fabric with the ruler markings at the required width. For example, to cut a 3"-wide strip, place the 3" ruler mark on the edge of the fabric.

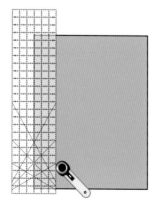

4. To cut squares, cut strips in the required widths. Trim the selvage ends of the strips. Align the left edge of the strips with the correct ruler markings. The sides of each square should have the same measurement as the width of the strips. Cut the strips into squares. Continue cutting squares until you have the number needed.

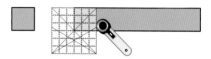

MACHINE PIECING

The quilts in this book are designed for easy rotary cutting and quick piecing. The most important thing to remember about machine piecing is that you need to maintain a consistent ¼"-wide seam allowance. Otherwise, the quilt blocks will not be the desired finished size. If that happens, the size of everything else in the quilt is affected, including alternate blocks, sashings, and borders. Measurements for all components of each quilt are based on blocks that finish accurately to the desired size plus ¼" on each edge for seam allowances.

Take the time to establish an exact ¼"-wide seam guide on your machine. Some machines have a special quilting foot that measures exactly ¼" from the center needle position to the edge of the foot. This feature allows you to use the edge of the presser foot to guide the fabric for a perfect ¼"-wide seam allowance. If your machine doesn't have such a foot, create a seam guide by placing the edge of a piece of tape, moleskin, or a magnetic seam guide ¼" away from the needle.

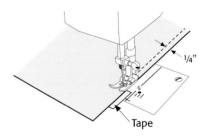

CHAIN PIECING

Chain piecing is an efficient system that saves time and thread. It's especially useful when you're making many identical units.

1. Sew the first pair of pieces from cut edge to cut edge, using 12 to 15 stitches per inch. At the end of the seam, stop sewing but do not cut the thread.

2. Feed the next pair of pieces under the presser foot, as close as possible to the first. Continue feeding pieces through the machine without cutting the threads between the pairs.

3. When all the pieces are sewn, remove the chain from the machine and clip the threads between the pairs of sewn pieces.

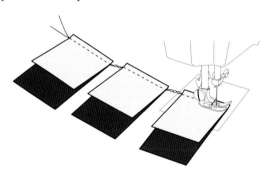

PRESSING

The traditional rule in quiltmaking is to press seams to one side, toward the darker color wherever possible. First press the seams flat from the wrong side of the fabric; then press the seams in the desired direction from the right side. Press carefully to avoid distorting the shapes.

When joining two seamed units, plan ahead and press the seam allowances in opposite directions as shown. This reduces bulk and makes it easier to match the seam lines. The seam allowances will butt against each other where two seams meet, making it easier to sew units with perfectly matched seam intersections.

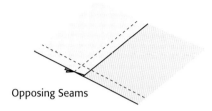

Opposing Seams

ASSEMBLING THE QUILT TOP

From squaring up your blocks so they are easier to sew together to adding borders that aren't wavy, you'll find all you need to know about assembling your quilt top in this section.

SQUARING UP BLOCKS

When your blocks are complete, take the time to square them up. Use a large, square ruler to measure your blocks and make sure they are the desired size plus an exact ¼" on each side for seam allowances. For example, if you are making 9" blocks, they should all measure 9½" before you sew them together. Trim the larger blocks to match the size of the smallest one. Be sure to trim all four sides; otherwise, your block will be lopsided.

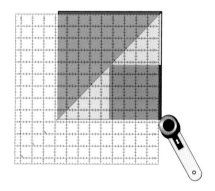

If your blocks are not the required finished size, adjust all the other components of the quilt, such as sashing and borders, accordingly.

ADDING BORDERS

For best results, do not cut border strips and sew them directly to the quilt without measuring first. The edges of a quilt often measure slightly longer than the distance through the quilt center, due to stretching during construction. Instead, measure the quilt top through the center in both directions to determine how long to cut the border strips. This step ensures that the finished quilt will be as straight and as "square" as possible, without wavy edges.

Many of the quilts in this book call for plain border strips. These strips are cut along the crosswise grain and seamed where extra length is needed.

Borders may have overlapped corners, corner squares, or mitered corners. Check the quilt pattern you are following to see which type of corner treatment you need.

Overlapped Corners

1. Measure the length of the quilt top through the center. From the crosswise grain, cut two border strips to that measurement, piecing as necessary. Determine the midpoints of the border and quilt top by folding them in half and creasing or pinning the centers. Then pin the borders to opposite sides of the quilt top, matching the center marks and ends and easing as necessary. Sew the border strips in place. Press the seams toward the borders.

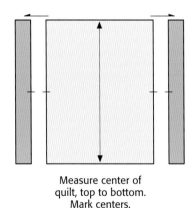

Measure center of
quilt, top to bottom.
Mark centers.

2. Measure the width of the quilt top through the center, including the side borders just added. From the crosswise grain, cut two border strips to that measurement, piecing as necessary. Mark the centers of the quilt edges and the border strips. Pin the borders to the top and bottom edges of the quilt top, matching the center marks and ends and easing as necessary. Sew the border strips in place. Press the seams toward the border.

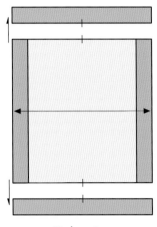

Mark centers.
Measure center of quilt, side to
side, including border strips.

PREPARING TO QUILT

If you'll be quilting your project by hand or on your home sewing machine, you'll want to follow the directions in this section for marking, layering, basting, and quilting. However, if you plan to have a professional machine quilter quilt your project, check with that person before preparing your finished quilt top in any way. Quilts do not need to be layered and basted for long-arm machine quilting, nor do they usually need to be marked.

MARKING THE QUILTING LINES

Whether you mark quilting designs on the quilt top or not depends upon the type of quilting you will be doing. Marking is not necessary if you plan to quilt in the ditch (along the seam lines) or outline quilt a uniform distance from seam lines. For more complex quilting designs, however, mark the quilt top before the quilt is layered with batting and backing.

Choose a marking tool that will be visible on your fabric and test it on fabric scraps to be sure the marks can be removed easily.

See "Marking tools" on page 71 for options. Masking tape can be used to mark straight quilting lines. Tape only small sections at a time and remove the tape when you stop at the end of the day; if tape is left on the quilt longer, the sticky residue may be difficult to remove from the fabric.

LAYERING AND BASTING THE QUILT

Once you complete the quilt top and mark it for quilting, assemble the quilt "sandwich," which consists of the backing, batting, and quilt top. The quilt backing and batting should be at least 4" larger than the quilt top. For large quilts, it is usually necessary to sew two or three lengths of fabric together to make a backing that is large enough. Trim away the selvages before piecing the lengths together. Press the seams open to make quilting easier.

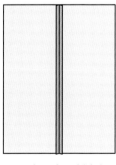
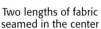

Two lengths of fabric seamed in the center

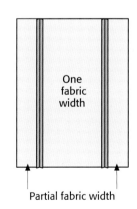

One fabric width

Partial fabric width

Batting comes packaged in standard bed sizes, or it can be purchased by the yard. Several weights or thicknesses are available. Thick battings are fine for tied quilts and comforters; a thinner batting is better, however, if you intend to quilt by hand or machine.

1. Spread the backing, wrong side up, on a flat, clean surface. Anchor it with pins or masking tape. Be careful not to stretch the backing out of shape.

2. Spread the batting over the backing, smoothing out any wrinkles.

3. Center the pressed quilt top, right side up, on top of the batting. Smooth out any wrinkles and make sure the quilt-top edges are parallel to the edges of the backing.

4. Starting in the center, baste with needle and thread and work diagonally to each corner. Then baste a grid of horizontal and vertical lines 6" to 8" apart. Finish by basting around the edges.

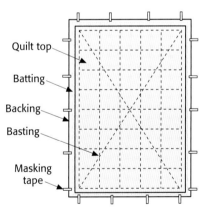

Quilt top

Batting

Backing

Basting

Masking tape

▶ **Note:** For machine quilting, you may baste the layers with No. 2 rustproof safety pins. Place pins about 6" to 8" apart, away from the areas you intend to quilt.

QUILTING TECHNIQUES

Some of the projects in this book were hand quilted, others were machine quilted, and some were quilted on long-arm quilting machines. The choice is yours!

HAND QUILTING

To quilt by hand, you will need short, sturdy needles (called "betweens"), quilting thread, and a thimble to fit the middle finger of your sewing hand. Most quilters also use a frame or hoop to support their work. Use the smallest needle you can comfortably handle; the finer the needle, the smaller your stitches will be. The basics of hand quilting are explained below. For more information on hand quilting, refer to *Loving Stitches: A Guide to Fine Hand Quilting* by Jeana Kimball (Martingale & Company, 2003).

1. Thread your needle with a single strand of quilting thread about 18" long. Make a small knot and insert the needle in the top layer about 1" from the place where you want to start stitching. Pull the needle out at the point where quilting will begin and gently pull the thread until the knot pops through the fabric and into the batting.

2. Take small, evenly spaced stitches through all three quilt layers. Rock the needle up and down through all layers, until you have three or four stitches on the needle. Place your other hand underneath the quilt so you can feel the needle point with the tip of your finger when a stitch is taken.

3. To end a line of quilting, make a small knot close to the last stitch; then backstitch, running the thread a needle's length through the batting. Gently pull the thread until the knot pops into the batting; clip the thread at the quilt's surface.

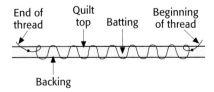

MACHINE QUILTING

Machine quilting is suitable for all types of quilts—from wall hangings to crib quilts to bed quilts. With machine quilting, you can quickly complete quilts that might otherwise languish on the shelves of your sewing room.

Marking the quilting design is only necessary if you need to follow a grid or a complex pattern. It is not necessary if you plan to quilt in the ditch, outline quilt a uniform distance from seam lines, or free-motion quilt in a random pattern.

For straight-line quilting, it is extremely helpful to have a walking foot to help feed the quilt layers through the machine without shifting or puckering. Some machines have a built-in walking foot; other machines require a separate attachment.

For free-motion quilting, you need a darning foot and the ability to drop or cover the feed dogs on your machine. With free-motion quilting, you guide the fabric in the direction of the design rather than turning the fabric under the needle. Use free-motion quilting to outline quilt a fabric motif or to create stippling or other curved designs.

LONG-ARM QUILTING

If you prefer to have the quilting done by a professional, ask at your local quilt shop for references about someone in your area who does this type of work. Generally, for long-arm quilting, you don't layer and baste the quilt prior to giving it to the quilter, nor do you have to mark the quilting designs. Often, however, the quilter will ask that you machine baste around the edges of the quilt for stability. Check with your long-arm professional to be sure of specifications regarding batting and backing sizes before cutting or piecing yours.

FINISHING

Bind your quilt, adding a hanging sleeve if you plan to hang your quilt, label it, and you're finished!

BINDING

For a French double-fold binding, cut strips 2" to 2½" wide across the width of the fabric. (Some quilters prefer narrow binding, especially if a low-loft batting is used. If you're using a thicker batting, you may want to usc 2½"-wide strips.) You will need enough strips to go around the perimeter of the quilt, plus 10" for seams and to turn the corners.

1. Sew the binding strips together to make one long strip. Join strips at right angles, right sides together, and stitch across the corner as shown. Trim excess fabric and press the seams open to make one long piece of binding.

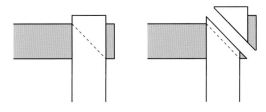

Joining Straight-Cut Strips

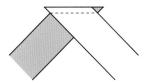

Joining Bias Strips

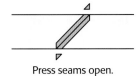

Press seams open.

2. Fold the strip in half lengthwise, wrong sides together, and press.

3. Trim the batting and backing even with the quilt top. If you plan to add a hanging sleeve, do so now before attaching the binding (see page 79).

4. Starting near the middle of one side of the quilt, align the raw edges of the binding with the raw edges of the quilt top. Using a walking foot and a ¼"-wide seam allowance, begin stitching the binding to the quilt, leaving a 6" tail unstitched. Stop stitching ¼" away from the corner of the quilt.

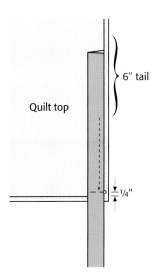

5. Lift the needle out of the quilt, and then turn the quilt so you will be stitching down the next side. Fold the binding up, away from the quilt, with the raw edges aligned. Fold the binding back down onto itself, even with the edge of the quilt top. Begin stitching ¼" from the corner, backstitching to secure the stitches. Repeat the process on the remaining edges and corners of the quilt.

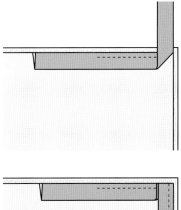

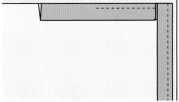

6. On the last side of the quilt, stop stitching about 7" from where you began. Overlap the end of the binding tail with the starting tail. Trim the binding ends with a perpendicular cut so the overlap is exactly the same distance as the cut width of your binding strips. (If your binding strips are 2½" wide, the overlap should be 2½"; for 2"-wide binding, the overlap should be 2".)

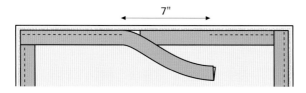

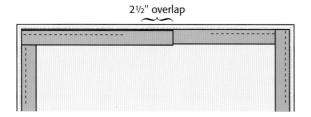

7. Open up the two ends of the folded binding. Place the tails right sides together so they join to form a right angle as shown. Pin the binding tails together, and then mark a diagonal stitching line from corner to corner.

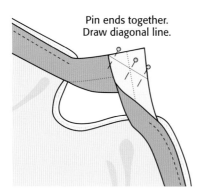

Pin ends together.
Draw diagonal line.

8. Stitch the binding tails together on the marked line. Trim the seam allowance to ¼"; press the seam open to reduce bulk. Refold the binding, align the edges with the raw edges of the quilt top, and finish sewing it in place.

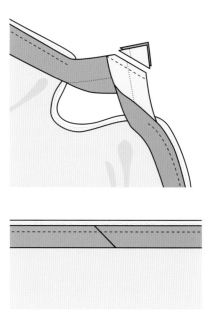

9. Fold the binding to the back of the quilt top to cover the machine stitching line. Hand stitch in place, mitering the corners.

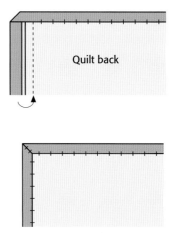

Quilt back

ADDING A HANGING SLEEVE

If you plan to display your finished quilt on the wall, be sure to add a hanging sleeve to hold the rod.

1. Using leftover fabric from the quilt backing, cut a strip 6" to 8" wide and 1" shorter than the width of your quilt. Fold the ends under ½", and then again ½" to make a hem. Stitch in place.

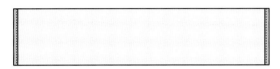

Fold ends under ½" twice.

2. Fold the fabric strip in half lengthwise, wrong sides together, and baste the raw edges to the top of the quilt back. The top edge of the sleeve will be secured when the binding is sewn on the quilt.

Baste sleeve to top edge of quilt.

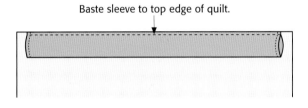

3. Finish the sleeve after the binding has been attached by blindstitching the bottom of the sleeve in place. Push the bottom edge of the sleeve up just a bit to provide a little give so the hanging rod does not put strain on the quilt.

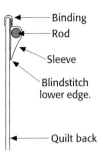

SIGNING YOUR QUILT

Future generations will be interested to know more than just who made the quilt and when, so be sure to include the name of the quilt, your name, your city and state, the date, the name of the recipient if the quilt is a gift, and any other interesting or important information about the quilt. The information can be handwritten, typed, or embroidered.

new and bestselling titles from

America's Best-Loved Craft & Hobby Books™

America's Best-Loved Quilt Books®

NEW RELEASES
1000 Great Quilt Blocks
American Stenciled Quilts
Americana Quilts
Appliquilt in the Cabin
Bed and Breakfast Quilts
Best of Black Mountain Quilts, The
Beyond the Blocks
Blissful Bath, The
Celebrations!
Color-Blend Appliqué
Fabulous Quilts from Favorite Patterns
Feathers That Fly
Handcrafted Garden Accents
Handprint Quilts
Knitted Throws and More for the Simply
    Beautiful Home
Knitter's Book of Finishing Techniques, The
Knitter's Template, A
Make Room for Christmas Quilts
More Paintbox Knits
Painted Whimsies
Patriotic Little Quilts
Quick Quilts Using Quick Bias
Quick-Change Quilts
Quilts for Mantels and More
Snuggle Up
Split-Diamond Dazzlers
Stack the Deck!
Strips and Strings
Sweet Dreams
Treasury of Rowan Knits, A
Triangle Tricks
Triangle-Free Quilts

APPLIQUÉ
Artful Album Quilts
Artful Appliqué
Blossoms in Winter
Easy Art of Appliqué, The
Fun with Sunbonnet Sue
Sunbonnet Sue All through the Year

BABY QUILTS
Easy Paper-Pieced Baby Quilts
Even More Quilts for Baby
More Quilts for Baby
Play Quilts
Quilted Nursery, The
Quilts for Baby

HOLIDAY QUILTS
Christmas at That Patchwork Place®
Christmas Cats and Dogs
Creepy Crafty Halloween
Handcrafted Christmas, A
Welcome to the North Pole

LEARNING TO QUILT
Joy of Quilting, The
Nickel Quilts
Quick Watercolor Quilts
Quilts from Aunt Amy
Simple Joys of Quilting, The
Your First Quilt Book (or it should be!)

PAPER PIECING
40 Bright and Bold Paper-Pieced Blocks
50 Fabulous Paper-Pieced Stars
For the Birds
Quilter's Ark, A
Rich Traditions

ROTARY CUTTING
101 Fabulous Rotary-Cut Quilts
365 Quilt Blocks a Year Perpetual Calendar
Around the Block Again
Around the Block with Judy Hopkins
Log Cabin Fever
More Fat Quarter Quilts

TOPICS IN QUILTMAKING
Batik Beauties
Frayed-Edge Fun
Log Cabin Fever
Machine Quilting Made Easy
Quick Watercolor Quilts
Reversible Quilts

CRAFTS
300 Papermaking Recipes
ABCs of Making Teddy Bears, The
Creating with Paint
Handcrafted Frames
Painted Chairs
Stamp in Color
Stamp with Style

KNITTING & CROCHET
365 Knitting Stitches a Year Perpetual
    Calendar
Clever Knits
Crochet for Babies and Toddlers
Crocheted Sweaters
Irresistible Knits
Knitted Shawls, Stoles, and Scarves
Knitted Sweaters for Every Season
Knitting with Novelty Yarns
Paintbox Knits
Simply Beautiful Sweaters
Simply Beautiful Sweaters for Men
Too Cute! Cotton Knits for Toddlers
Ultimate Knitter's Guide, The

Our books are available at bookstores and your favorite craft, fabric, and yarn
retailers. If you don't see the title you're looking for, visit us at
www.martingale-pub.com or contact us at:

1-800-426-3126
International: 1-425-483-3313

Fax: 1-425-486-7596

E-mail: info@martingale-pub.com

For more information and a full list of our titles, visit our Web site.